DISCARD

Centerville Library
Washington-Centerville Public Library
Centerville, Ohio

W9-BAT-398

GROW.
COOK.
PRESERVE.

GROW. COOK. PRESERVE.

THE COMPLETE GUIDE TO SUSTAINABLE FOOD

HELEN LYNNE CULPEPPER

Aadamsmedia

AVON, MASSACHUSETTS

Copyright © 2015 by F+W Media, Inc.
All rights reserved.
This book, or parts thereof, may not be reproduced in any form without permission from the publisher; exceptions are made for brief excerpts used in published reviews.

Published by Adams Media, a division of F+W Media, Inc.
57 Littlefield Street, Avon, MA 02322. U.S.A.
www.adamsmedia.com

Contains material adapted and abridged from *The Everything® Grow Your Own Vegetables Book* by Catherine Abbott, copyright © 2010 by F+W Media, Inc., ISBN 10: 1-4405-0013-4, ISBN 13: 978-1-4405-0013-8; *The Everything® Root Cellaring Book* by Catherine Abbott, copyright © 2011 by F+W Media, Inc., ISBN 10: 1-4405-0468-7, ISBN 13: 978-1-4405-0468-6; *The Everything® Canning and Preserving Book* by Patricia Telesco, copyright © 2009 by F+W Media, Inc., ISBN 10: 1-59869-987-3, ISBN 13: 978-1-59869-987-6; *The Year-Round Harvest* by Catherine Abbott and Alison Woitunski, copyright © 2012 by F+W Media, Inc., ISBN 10: 1-4405-2816-0, ISBN 13: 978-1-4405-2816-3; and *The Everything® Vegan Cookbook* by Jolinda Hackett, copyright © 2010 by F+W Media, Inc., ISBN 10: 1-4405-0216-1, ISBN 13: 978-1-4405-0216-3.

ISBN 10: 1-4405-8481-8
ISBN 13: 978-1-4405-8481-7
eISBN 10: 1-4405-8482-6
eISBN 13: 978-1-4405-8482-4

Printed in the United States of America.

10   9   8   7   6   5   4   3   2   1

Library of Congress Cataloging-in-Publication Data

Culpepper, Helen Lynne.
    Grow. cook. preserve. / Helen Lynne Culpepper.
        pages cm
    Includes index.
     ISBN 978-1-4405-8481-7 (pob) -- ISBN 1-4405-8481-8 (pob) -- ISBN 978-1-4405-8482-4 (ebook) -- ISBN 1-4405-8482-6 (ebook)
        1. Cooking (Vegetables) 2. Cooking (Fruit) 3. Cooking (Herbs) 4. Vegetable gardening. I. Title.
    TX801.C855 2014
    641.6'5--dc23

                    2014028895

Many of the designations used by manufacturers and sellers to distinguish their products are claimed as trademarks. Where those designations appear in this book and F+W Media, Inc. was aware of a trademark claim, the designations have been printed with initial capital letters.

Always follow safety and commonsense cooking protocol while using kitchen utensils, operating ovens and stoves, and handling uncooked food. If children are assisting in the preparation of any recipe, they should always be supervised by an adult.

Cover design by Elisabeth Lariviere.

Cover images © iStockphoto.com/g_muradin, iStockphoto.com/3DMaster, iStockphoto.com/Olga_Varlamova.

Interior illustrations by Barry Littman and Eric Andrews.

This book is available at quantity discounts for bulk purchases. For information, please call 1-800-289-0963.

CONTENTS

CHAPTER 4 **FRUITS AND HERBS**

Fruits

Herbs

PART 3: Preserve and Store. 169

CHAPTER 5 **WHERE TO STORE**. 171

The Root Cellar 172

Unconventional Storage Spaces. 180

Root-Cellar Conditions 183

Pits and Trenches 185

Vegetable Storage 187

CHAPTER 6 **CAN AND PRESERVE**. 189

Determining the Best Preservation Method 190

Canning 190

Drying. 195

Freezing 197

Pickling 201

Fermentation 203

INTRODUCTION

Do you wish you could serve your family fresh, farm-to-table meals instead of heating up yet another frozen dinner? Are you tired of countless trips to the grocery store where you spend too much money on food you don't really want to eat? Concerned about what those prepackaged meals are doing to the environment?

If you're looking for a better way to feed your family, you've taken the first step. *Grow. Cook. Preserve.* teaches you everything you need to know to lower your carbon footprint and feed your family inexpensive, sustainable, delicious meals made from ingredients that you grew in your own garden.

Throughout the book you'll find more than 150 recipes that teach you how to prepare and preserve delightfully rustic dishes such as Spicy Sweet Cucumber Salad, Dried Tomato Risotto with Spinach and Pine Nuts, Blueberry Cobbler, and more. In addition, Part 1 details everything you need to get ready to grow your own foods, including information on what types of plants to grow, where to plant, and how to troubleshoot any issues. Part 2 teaches you how to choose and cook the fruits, veggies, and herbs that will flourish in your garden. And Part 3 provides detailed information on how to preserve and store your garden's bounty so you can enjoy it year-round.

So whether you want to leave the grocery store behind for good or just have more input into what you're putting on your table, *Grow. Cook. Preserve.* gives you what you need to get your hands dirty and then eat up the fruits of your labor. Enjoy!

PART 1

GET READY

CHAPTER 1

KNOW BEFORE YOU GROW

TO truly experience the self-sufficiency of farm-to-table food, you need to grow your own fruits and veggies. But how can you make sure your garden will be successful? Sunlight, water, and soil are the key ingredients to a productive garden. Depending on the area you have to work with, the quality and quantity of these components can differ widely and can affect how you design your garden. Other factors, such as wind, pests, drainage, and space, can also affect how and what you can grow. Understanding the strengths and challenges of your outdoor space is the first step to planning a successful garden. By maximizing strengths, thinking creatively, and viewing challenges as guidelines rather than limitations, your garden will be a unique reflection of your home and personality as well as an optimum growing environment that gives you amazing, homegrown food when you need it.

SUNLIGHT

Open sunlight for your garden is your top priority when deciding where to plant. Although not all crops require the same amount of sunlight, the majority of your plants will need direct sunlight for at least six hours a day during the height of their growth.

GARDENING IN A LARGER SPACE

If you have a yard or an outdoor space large enough to provide you with options for garden placement, then chances are you already have some idea as to where you would like to put your garden. There might be a spot in the yard that looks too vacant, or an area that you could access easily from the kitchen. Maybe you want the garden to be near an outdoor eating area or a space where your children like to play. When determining the consistency and directness of sunlight for your garden placement, you will want to observe the location you have in mind, but choose some other sites to observe as well.

By pinpointing and observing multiple sites, you can better gauge the quality of sunlight in each area. One spot might seem sunny enough on its own, but when compared to a different section of your outdoor space, you may notice that the sunlight in your spot is less present at certain times throughout the day, or that there is more consistent shade than you expected. It could turn out that the area that you were imagining for your garden is not the best option, but if you observe a few different locations at once, you'll be able to adapt your plans.

SUN IN A SMALL SPACE

If there isn't much option for where your garden can go—for example, if you have a very small yard, patio, deck, or an assigned community garden plot—then the goal of making your growing-site observations is to understand the type of sunlight your garden has access to. Being familiar with this beforehand will allow you to plant strategically. When observing your space, you want to determine if your garden area receives mostly direct sunlight, mostly shade, or a combination of both. Once you determine which category your garden space fits into, you can plant crops that will thrive in your particular environment.

Tree Cover and Shade-Producing Vegetation

Depending on the time of year you are making your observations, pay attention to trees and other vegetation that may not be in bloom but will have shade-producing foliage during the growing season. Nearby trees do not always rule out a potential garden location, but it is important to understand the scope of the shade they will produce. Knowing the type of tree or vegetation and assessing its relative health will help you to understand how much shade will be provided. If the area and the vegetation are new to you, talking to neighbors who are familiar with the specific tree or site is often the simplest way to get an idea of how much shade to expect. If you are unable to get the information you need from the folks living around you, a little research and common sense should be enough to give you a basic idea of how much shade to expect. If your outdoor space is tree-heavy, don't despair; often, pruning a few branches or cutting back some vegetation can open up plenty of sunlight for a productive garden.

Take a Sunlight Survey

It will be easiest to make accurate assumptions about sunlight at times of the year when there is ample daylight and also during days when the sun is visible and present. For some this will mean that the fall and early spring will be the best times to observe potential garden sites (other than during the growing season itself) and also on a day when the sun is out. This might mean that you have to make observations over a span of several days if you're planning your garden at a time of year when sunlight is scarce or unpredictable.

In general, making observations at specific points throughout the day will allow you to accurately assess your access to sunlight. You can stagger these observations over a larger window of time by observing the garden site at different times on different days if you are unable to take note of the light at every hour (beginning in the morning until early evening) during a single day. Depending on where your garden is located in relation to where you live and work, it might take several days to develop a complete understanding of the sunlight in your garden site.

If one area was fully immersed in sunlight during one-third of the day, but without any direct sun for the remaining two-thirds, this area does not have consistent sunlight despite receiving some direct light. A site that received partial to full sun throughout all times of the day, but did not reach a point of receiving direct sunlight, has more consistency of sunlight but less direct sunlight. In an ideal situation, you do not need to choose between planting a garden in direct or consistent sunlight, as both direct and consistent sunlight would be present, although this is not always the reality.

Choosing a garden site that has a balance of consistent and direct light is important, but this variable is also flexible and the end balance will be different in each garden. There are benefits and challenges to the type of sunlight that your garden receives, and it is important to consider how the variable of sunlight will interact with the other components of your garden. For example, a garden without any shade will require more water, whereas a garden that receives partial shade in the afternoon will use its water more efficiently. Likewise, a garden that gets too much shade might be more susceptible to fungus or mold growth in the soil. As you move through the steps of site assessment, you will continue to gather information about all the variables important to your garden. By the end of this chapter you will have an understanding of how all of these components interact with one another.

WATER

Where your water access is and the size of your garden are important factors in determining garden site location. If you are planning to water your garden with a fixed irrigation setup, such as drip tape, a sprinkler system, or any other stationary system, your primary limiting factor is the length of your connecting equipment (typically a hose) and the area that this connection will have to cross in order to get to the garden. Your garden should not be any farther than your connection can realistically reach. For some gardeners, this means paying attention to any terrain or obstacles that are not ideal to extend a hose across. A driveway, children's play area, or a heavily trafficked walkway or stairway are some areas you might want to avoid laying a hose or irrigation line across.

RAIN BARRELS

Creating a system to catch and conserve rainwater is the most inexpensive and self-sufficient way to water your garden (other than relying on the rain itself). Depending on where you live and where your garden is located, this may or may not be practical. If possible, you will want to build a system that captures rainwater and transports it into a rain barrel where you can then decide when and how to release the water.

A basic rain-catch system uses tubing to capture rainwater from the gutters of your house, garage, or other buildings, and transports this water into a storage container that is elevated above the level of your garden. From this container, a hose or additional tubing can be connected to a water-release spigot that can be opened or closed. Although the pressure of the water from a simple rain-barrel system is not great enough to use with a sprinkler system, the rain barrel in this system can easily be integrated with drip-tape irrigation or used to fill a watering can.

If you plan to build a rain-barrel system to irrigate your crops, you will want your garden to be located at a level lower than the rain barrel and within a reasonable distance. You can usually accomplish this elevation difference by positioning your barrel on a stand or blocks, putting it at a higher level than the garden. It is important to keep in mind that a typical rain barrel will not have enough pressure to force water quickly through the irrigation line. The watering process in this system will be a slow one, but if built effectively, it will make irrigation efficient and require only very light lifting for the gardener. You can plan on having to open your water spigot and wait several hours or even days (depending on the size of your garden) for the entire garden to be watered, but the only effort required from you will be turning the spigot on and off, and observing the plot to see when enough water has been distributed. The more hosing and irrigation line that the water has to travel through (how far away the garden is from the rain-barrel system and how much tubing is used within the system), the greater amount of time watering takes.

HAND WATERING

If you plan to water your garden by hand, either by filling a watering can or by extending a hose for each watering, it is particularly important that your garden be a reasonable distance from your water source. Even for the gardener with the best of intentions, a garden that is more than a quick walk away from a water source will most likely not be watered with as much attention and care as it would if water were easily accessible. This can translate into overwatering for some crops and underwatering for others if all plants are given the same amount of water at the same time because of the amount of effort an individual watering can take. By asking yourself the following questions, you will be able to think critically about how much distance from the water source to your garden is too far.

- On a daily basis, how much time are you willing and able to dedicate to watering your garden?
- If uncoiling and recoiling a hose will happen for each watering, how long is the hose and how much time and effort will be needed to extend it?
- How many times will you need to fill and refill your watering can to complete one garden watering?
- How heavy is a full watering can and how much is a reasonable amount of walking back and forth?

Many factors will affect how often your garden will need to be watered. How well the soil retains moisture and how sunny or wet of a growing season you have can drastically alter your watering schedule. Some growing seasons your garden may only need watering a few times during the entire season, and other summers you may find yourself watering every evening for several weeks. Depending on where you live, some of these factors might be predictable, and others may not be.

SOIL

The foundation of self-sufficient gardening is healthy soil. If you remember the mantra "A good gardener grows healthy soil and healthy soil grows healthy plants," and treat your soil accordingly, your crops will not only be productive but they will be highly nutritious as well. Because soil is the foundation of your garden, understanding the composition and characteristics of the soil you are working with is crucial for both short-term and long-term garden health. In order to properly assess your growing site, you will need to assess your soil.

SOIL TESTING

In urban and suburban areas, lead and heavy-metal contamination is a very real concern. If you are planning to garden directly in soil that is already present in your yard or outdoor space, you will want to test your soil before planting anything. Often the easiest way to do this is to contact the nearest state university to find out what your testing options are.

The Department of Plant, Soil, and Insect Sciences at the University of Massachusetts, for example, accepts and tests soil samples from home gardeners and commercial farmers at a minimal cost. In addition to testing for dangerous contaminants such as lead, this particular test also addresses soil health and productivity, providing the grower with specific information about what will grow best and any amendments to the soil that should or could be made. The turnaround time for the results is typically less than two weeks, and all you need in order to take samples are a small trowel, zip-top bags, and a marker for labeling. To learn the exact steps and to print a soil sample order form, visit *www.umass.edu/soiltest*. The information you receive from a soil test can often be the equivalent of knowledge that would otherwise take years to only partially understand.

Once you determine whether or not your existing soil is safe to plant in, you are equipped to decide whether to use raised beds as a cap for contaminated soil, or to plant directly in the ground in safe soil. Keep in mind that even if you already know that you want to go with a raised-bed approach, you still need to test your soil. Some soil can have heavy-metal levels high enough to warrant safeguards in addition to using raised beds. In some cases, you might decide that container gardening, which is explained later on in this chapter, is the best approach.

HOW TO GROW?

Once you've figured out where you want to grow your fruits, veggies, and herbs, you need to figure out how you'd like to grow them. Raised beds are an option as are various containers that guarantee healthy soil.

RAISED BEDS

Wood-framed raised beds are a common feature in urban and suburban gardening. Not only do they offer protection from soil contamination, they also provide a tidy appearance, can be sized to fit in all different types of outdoor environments, and are easy to build. Raised-bed frames can be assembled at as much cost as you would like to put into the project. Depending on how particular you are about appearance, you can use any dimensional lumber that you already have, or you can purchase lumber that meets your specifications at your nearest lumberyard. As long as the wood has not been chemically or pressure-treated, it will suffice for building. The only other materials you will need for the frame are basic hardware (screws, nail, brackets) and a drill or hammer.

Raised Beds

To fill raised beds, you will need to purchase soil or finished compost. This is often the most limiting factor because it can be expensive to purchase this much soil. But by doing a little research, you can avoid spending big bucks at your local garden center. Find out if there are any local composting facilities or other agriculture operations that will sell you unbagged soil or finished compost at a lower cost. If you have access to a pickup truck and can go get the soil or compost yourself, you can save even more money by eliminating any delivery charges. To give you an idea of how much soil you will need, a standard 12-inch-deep, 8-foot by 4-foot raised bed will need 32 cubic feet of soil.

Framed raised beds are perfect for yards that do not have one open space large enough for an entire garden. Using raised beds allows you to break up what would normally comprise one garden space, and spread out the different components over your entire outdoor area. For people who have limited outdoor space and/or yards with a diverse terrain and spotty sun coverage, framed raised beds offer versatility and a way to make the most of limited space.

GROW.

Working with your existing soil is the best idea if it is safe and healthy soil to plant in and you have enough open space to do so. If you own the land that you are gardening, or are planning to garden on this land for at least several years, you will be able to undertake the care needed for long-term soil amendments that will make working with your existing soil worthwhile. When you get ready to prep your soil, which is discussed in the next chapter, it will be important to have an understanding of the basic characteristics of the soil you are working with. The easiest way to do this (in addition to reading the results from your soil test) is to dig around in your potential garden site. Is the soil rocky? Does it remind you more of clay or sand? Do you notice any worms or insect life?

CONTAINER GARDENING

Using container gardens to grow food is not only practical but also a fast and easy way to enhance the aesthetics of any yard, deck, or other outdoor space quickly and inexpensively. Whether you live someplace where your only option is to grow food in containers, or you haven't the time or desire to convert your yard into a mini-farm, using containers to grow food is an easy way to quickly establish a garden just about anywhere.

When to Use

Container gardening can be a highly productive way to grow food when you don't have access to much outdoor space or healthy soil. Building inexpensive containers is easy, and you can adapt containers for vertical growing. Containers also can be relocated in your outdoor space as necessary to achieve optimal conditions for your crops. If bad backs or other physical limitations are a concern, you will want to seriously consider using containers because of the flexibility in height and location that they provide.

Some vegetables have a shallow root system; others have much deeper roots and need more space to grow. When choosing containers for your vegetables, there are three important rules to remember: First, the container must be deep enough to hold enough soil to accommodate the plant's root growth. Second, it must be large enough for the plant to grow to maturity. And finally, water must be able to drain easily from the bottom of the container so the soil does not get waterlogged. The container can be any shape so long as it can fulfill these three essentials.

Common container gardens are comprised of basic pots and planters that you can buy at any garden center. For the gardener wanting to grow food more intensively, however, these containers can be limiting. A plastic storage tote with a lid is a good choice for container gardening. A typical 20-gallon tote is at least 12 inches deep, allowing for root space. By drilling drainage holes in the bottom of the tote, water can easily drain out so plant roots don't become waterlogged. If the tote container is elevated a few inches, the lid can be used as a drainage catch tray beneath it. You can also use a container that you already have on hand; reusing an old wheelbarrow or other household item can be a great way to avoid spending more money, find a new use for an old object, and even create a decorative display.

WHAT TO GROW

Deciding what to grow is one of the most exciting parts of planning your garden, but before you start growing, you want to consider your local climate and what you actually like to eat! Think beyond the summer months of freshly picked salad items, all the way to what type of pumpkins you want to carve for Halloween, what you like to eat on Thanksgiving, and other favorite meals during the winter holidays and cold weather. Once you determine what you want to eat, what your storage options are, and which foods your household consumes the most of, you'll be ready to decide exactly what to grow in your garden. If you plan and plant correctly, your harvest will sustain you year-round.

CONSIDER HARDINESS PLANT ZONES

Hardiness plant zones are growing zones based on the average annual minimum temperature of an area. The U.S. Department of Agriculture (USDA) divides North America into eleven zones based on temperature. In order to understand the hardiness of certain plants, when to plant, the best varieties for your garden, and how to care for plants throughout the colder months, you need to know which hardiness zone you are growing in. Take a look at the following zone map and figure out what you'd like to plant and when you need to get those seeds into the ground.

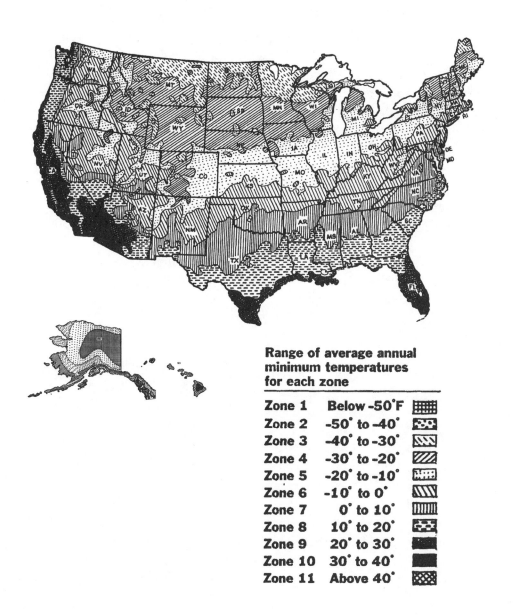

**Range of average annual
minimum temperatures
for each zone**

Zone 1	Below –50°F
Zone 2	–50° to –40°
Zone 3	–40° to –30°
Zone 4	–30° to –20°
Zone 5	–20° to –10°
Zone 6	–10° to 0°
Zone 7	0° to 10°
Zone 8	10° to 20°
Zone 9	20° to 30°
Zone 10	30° to 40°
Zone 11	Above 40°

Hardiness Plant Zone Map

KNOW THE GROWING PERIOD

It's important to understand the growing period for the fruits, veggies, and herbs that you will plant. All plants fall into a few different categories of life cycles. Depending on whether or not a plant is an annual, biennial, perennial, or an evergreen, you can expect your plants to require different sorts of care, and to vary in whether they need to be replanted every year or if they will last longer than one season. Knowing how long certain plants will produce will help you plan your garden not only for your first season but also for seasons to come.

Annual

Annuals are plants that live for only one season—flowering, fruiting, and then dying at the end of this process. The length of this season depends on the specific plant. It is usually a good idea to stagger plantings of annuals that have a shorter season in order to produce a continuous supply for as long as possible. Some commonly planted annuals include:

- Beans
- Eggplants
- Lettuce
- Melons
- Onions
- Parsnips
- Peppers
- Potatoes
- Squash

It is interesting to note that some food plants that are actually perennials or biennials are grown as annuals, either for convenience or because they won't survive the colder months. Carrots are actually biennials and tomatoes are true perennials, yet both are commonly grown as annuals.

Biennial

Biennial plants are those that live for two seasons. These plants will not fruit until their second and final season. They often are planted as annuals because of the inconvenience that a biennial plant can pose to gardeners who cannot harvest the whole plant until after the seed has been dropped. Biennials include:

- Beets
- Brussels sprouts
- Cabbage
- Caraway
- Carrots
- Celery
- Evening primrose
- Parsley
- Turnips

Perennial

Easily the most cost-effective plants to grow and harvest, true perennials live almost indefinitely and return every spring. Some varieties of lesser strength, however, will eventually die off. The length of these plants' lives can be affected by different factors of care and climate. Some perennials propagate via their underground roots or bulb systems. Some favorite perennials (though not in all hardiness zones) include:

- Artichokes
- Blueberries
- Chives
- Lemon balm
- Lemongrass
- Marjoram
- Oregano
- Raspberries
- Rhubarb
- Rosemary
- Sage
- Sun choke
- Tarragon
- Thyme

Evergreen

Evergreen herbs keep their leaves year-round. Depending on the specific plant and the growing zone you live in, this might mean that you can leave your evergreen herbs outdoors all winter. In some zones you will need to cover and protect your evergreen herbs, and in zones with the harshest winters, you will have to bring them inside during the colder months if you wish to maintain the same plant for the next season. Evergreen herbs do require pruning, but if you are using them to cook with, then regular harvesting should take care of this. Some common evergreen herbs include:

- Lavender
- Oregano
- Rosemary
- Savory
- Thyme

WHAT DO YOU WANT TO EAT?

It's easy to decide what you want to plant by thinking about what you and your family will actually eat. After all, you don't want to plant an entire garden of beans if no one in your family will eat them! A great way to do this is to think about your whole diet throughout the year and how what you plant now will keep you eating sustainable favorites when you want them. A fun way to start this process is to break down your favorite meal into its plant-derived ingredients and see which ones you can grow at home. You'll be surprised at how many of the ingredients can easily come from your own garden. You might not be able to grow the peppercorn in your favorite sauce recipe, but you can certainly grow the tomatoes, onions, garlic, basil, and oregano.

Every household uses some foods more regularly than others throughout the year. In how many meals a day or a week do you use garlic or onion? Is there a favorite recipe that calls for a certain herb? What are you most likely to throw together when you're in a rush—is it a pasta-and-sauce dish or rice and beans? Do you eat a lot of spicy food? Think about the things you cook with and eat most often. Chances are, if you look around your kitchen right now, they're already on the shelves and in the cabinets that are most easily accessible.

Once you have an idea of the storage and cooking qualities that are important to you for each type of food, you're ready to put your crops into the categories that will translate into dishes you'll cook at home throughout the year. In order to have a well-balanced and diverse diet, you'll want to include things from most of the following categories. It's up to you to adjust how much of each you want to grow. Based on your tastes and unique needs, you might find yourself focusing more on some food types than others. It is okay to do this as long as you keep in mind that come winter, you're more likely to be happy with your diet if there's a good diversity of food.

Greens

Spicy salad mix, purple heirloom lettuce, arugula, spinach, frisée—the salad list is long and fresh greens are satisfying and easy to grow. Direct seeding is almost always successful, and the plants germinate and mature quickly, allowing you to try many different types throughout the season. Many types of greens can germinate in and withstand colder weather. This means that, depending upon your growing zone and your ability to shelter your crops, you can plan on fresh greens beyond the first frost. If you love your greens, it is important to include a variety that allows for fresh consumption as long as the season allows, and also for greens that you can enjoy in a preserved form. If you're new to the wide world of greens, consult any seed catalog to get ideas. Johnny's Selected Seeds catalog is a great resource that is sure to get you excited about your greens.

Tomatoes

No other garden product is so poorly represented by the grocery-store version. The world of tomatoes is a large one, and certain tomatoes are better used for different purposes. Slicing tomatoes are served fresh with slices of cheese, in a sandwich, or in a salad. San Marzano tomatoes, a variety of plum tomatoes, are famous for Italian-style sweet sauces. Other tomatoes with more meat and less water, such as Romas, are best for canning, dehydrating, or making paste. Cherry varieties are fun, but are generally difficult to store and cook with; they are best used fresh. Make a list of what you would like to do with your tomatoes and then choose the varieties that will meet these needs. Depending on how much space you have for planting and storing, it's a good idea to start with one type of tomato for each different use.

Root Vegetables

Root vegetables and squash are easy to grow, preserve, and include in your homemade dishes. Potatoes, onions, garlic, carrots, celeriac, rutabaga, turnips, radishes, kohlrabi, shallots, Jerusalem artichokes, sweet potatoes, swedes (rutabaga, or Swedish turnip), and cassava are enough to fill any root cellar. Depending on your style of gardening, a good idea is to choose your favorite root vegetables and then supplement these with ones you would like to try. If you've never tasted a parsnip, you probably don't want to give them half of your garden space. Potatoes alone are an incredibly versatile vegetable; there are literally thousands of varieties, with extreme differences in tastes and colors. Plant potatoes in a variety of colors—red, gold, purple, and even orange. Harvesting potatoes is like going on an Easter egg hunt, and between the fun of digging them up and the beautifully bright colors, it will be easy to get your family eating potatoes in a form other than French fries.

Beans and Other Legumes

Beans will grow in almost any reasonably good garden soil. They grow best in a sandy, loamy soil with a neutral pH (acidity/alkalinity level). Beans do not like a lot of moisture before they germinate, but they do need regular watering once they have sprouted to produce tender beans. They are best harvested young when they are the most tender and need to be picked every few days so the plant knows it needs to keep producing more. If you leave the pods on the plant, the plant will take it as a sign to stop producing.

Brassicas (Cabbage, Broccoli, Kale, and Brussels Sprouts)

Any of the brassicas are a good choice if you are hoping to eat fresh foods during the winter. Cabbage, kale, and Brussels sprouts do well in the ground up until the first frost. They also store well in your root cellar and can be enjoyed fresh for many months. Incorporating a taste of green Brussels sprouts or crispy raw cabbage will make your family's winter meals more colorful and fresh.

Herbs

Herbs are hugely important if you care about flavor! The herbs that you grow yourself will have a stronger flavor than any herbs from a store. Herbs are also important because of their aromatic and medicinal qualities. Think about all the ways that you can use herbs—as tea, to make your home smell pleasant, to soothe coughs and colds, or to flavor your favorite dishes. Having a variety of herbs in your garden and diet will add fun, health, and flavor to the winter months and meals.

Squash and Pumpkins

Not only are squash and pumpkins great for storing, but they also mark the seasons in a way that other foods do not. In addition to the nutritional value and versatility that cooking and consuming squash provides, it's fun for younger family members to grow their very own Halloween pumpkins. And don't forget about favorites like sweet potato and pumpkin pies! Squash dishes are important to holiday meals for a reason—they are actually in season during the fall and winter holidays. Squash and pumpkins do produce a significant amount of foliage per plant and also take up quite a bit of root-cellar space. This does not mean that gardeners working with a small space can't plant and store squash and pumpkins; you can, but you will have to be experimental and creative.

PRESERVE.

In order to get the most use and longevity out of the pumpkins and winter squash that you grow, it's important to cure these veggies after you harvest them. Cut the stems to the woody section, about 4 inches long, and allow the pumpkin or squash to stay in a dry, well-ventilated area for at least a week. After they have been cured, squash and pumpkins will last for months in root storage; otherwise they can actually start to rot within just a few weeks of being picked. If you harvest your jack-o'-lantern pumpkin in early September, make sure to cure it so that it lasts until Halloween!

Peppers (Hot and Sweet)

If you like peppers, growing many different kinds is easy to do. Hot peppers add a spicy component to favorite meals, and for some people, cooking with hot peppers and spice is a must. Even if you aren't a fan of spicy foods, growing and storing some hot peppers is important as a way to add versatility and depth to your cooking and eating. Sweet peppers come in many varieties that are excellent when added to family favorites such as pizza or fajitas.

SUSTAINABLE FOOD

Growing and planning a garden because you want to live a sustainable lifestyle means changing your gardening mindset. Instead of planting and growing only the things you like to eat fresh in the summer—often salad ingredients such as tomatoes and lettuce— you'll also need to grow staple crops that you're used to purchasing in bulk from the grocery store. It's exciting to learn that you can grow and store these foods yourself, but it requires careful planning and forethought. In order to grow and store the best food for you and your family's diet, it's important to remember the basics: Grow the foods that are the backbone and staples of your kitchen, as well as try new foods and new varieties of old favorites to maintain an element of excitement.

CHAPTER 2

TROUBLESHOOTING AND DAMAGE CONTROL

Now that you know what you want to grow and where, how can you make sure you're not tossing out your healthy, sustainable lifestyle and heading right back to the grocery store? Two words: damage control. In this chapter, you'll learn how important it is to compost, how to make sure you give your plants the water they need, plus get information on companion planting, pest control, staking, starting seeds, and more! If you're going to all the effort of growing the food to use in the rustic recipes later on in the book, you want to make sure the fruits of your labor end up in something delicious . . . instead of in the compost pile.

COMPOSTING

Compost is an important part of any gardening system. It does take some time and effort to get used to composting if it isn't already part of your lifestyle, but the rewards are worth it. Not only is composting a constructive way to use your kitchen waste and keep your garden site organized and free of debris, but adding compost to your soil increases productivity and soil health. There are many different methods of composting, and choosing the best one for you and your family will help to make composting an integral part of your family's routine and your garden's cycle.

Composting has experienced a surge in popularity, so the home gardener has many choices of bins. The type of bin you choose will depend on where it will be located, how much waste you will have, and how much time and energy you want to put toward making compost. The following methods described all involve using a large bin that will typically live outdoors. In the case of a worm bin, however, during some times of the year the worms will need to be warmer and will have to live in your garage, basement, or some other sheltered area.

WORM COMPOSTING

If you live in an apartment or condominium and do not have access to a backyard, composting with earthworms—a process known as vermiculture—can be an easy way to turn your kitchen waste into a nutrient-rich compost you can add to your garden. An earthworm has the ability to consume its own weight in soil and organic matter each day. It leaves behind castings that form a rich compost. A pound of earthworms will generally compost one pound of kitchen waste per day. It is also easy to build your own worm-composting container.

The easiest way to build a worm bin to hold your earthworms is to use a standard 20-gallon/76-liter storage bin with a lid (the same kind described for use as a container garden).

1. Drill a line of small air holes around the top perimeter of the bin and in the lid itself for airflow.
2. Drill a larger drainage hole in the bottom front of the bin, and attach tubing using a waterproof sealant to glue in place. This tubing will catch the liquid from the worm castings, so you will also want to design a way to keep the tube elevated or closed until you want to access this "worm tea" to add to your garden.

There are several ways you can construct the interior of your worm bin, but I have found success using a tray system inside the plastic bin. Using this tray method, place two stacking perforated storage trays or drawers (the type you often see in bathrooms or on a desk) inside the bin, stacked on top of each other. Your worms will live in the bottom tray and will migrate to the top tray in search of food once they have consumed the contents of the bottom tray. By relocating to the top tray when all the food has been eaten in the bottom tray, the worms will separate themselves from their castings, as the castings will remain in the bottom tray, ready to be emptied out into your garden. After you add the castings to your garden, you can then place the emptied tray on top of the tray that now contains your worms and kitchen waste. Continue this rotation every time the bottom tray fills up and is processed into nutrient-rich castings. The bottom of the storage bin will slowly fill with worm tea, and you can use the drainage hole to access this powerful fertilizer when enough accumulates.

GROW.

To access worm tea from your bin, you can easily fashion a simple system made from drainage tubing long enough to attach to the lid with a string. When you want to drain the worm tea, merely untie the string and let the liquid flow out the tube. If you don't like the looks of this more basic model, you can attach a spigot that can be turned on and off to allow the liquid to drain out. Note that you will have to wait for a lot of worm tea to accumulate for this spigot method to be worth the effort.

What You Need to Know about Worms

When you install your tray system inside the bin, you will want to create a simple worm habitat in the bottom bin. By adding a layer of newspaper, then soil or compost, and a layer of shredded newspaper, your worms will be ready to go!

The best worms for your worm bin are a type called red wigglers. You can purchase these at some garden centers and can also order them online; or if you have the time and energy, you can find them in your yard. You don't need very many to get started because they reproduce quickly to match their food supply. But you will need to carefully monitor your worm population and slowly increase their food supply so that the food supply is in balance with the number of worms in your bin—you don't want one to outmatch the other. Red wigglers can process most food waste, but you cannot feed them citrus, meat, bones, or dairy products. You can also add shredded newspaper and dryer lint to create a healthy, odor-free habitat.

THREE-BIN SYSTEM COMPOSTING

Constructing your own bin can save you money. You can use recycled materials, and make the bin the size that will best fit your needs. One common construction is a three-bin wood and wire system. It is designed to provide good air circulation, and each bin is usually 3 feet by 3 feet—the minimum size you need to make good compost. The first bin is used to collect debris, the second bin is where you start your pile, and the third bin is where you put the compost pile when it is nearly finished. This kind of structure will last a long time if you use rot-resistant wood such as cedar or redwood (not pressure-treated lumber).

Wire fencing or wire mesh can be used to make a compost bin so long as the holes are small enough to hold the materials you have. Bending the wire into a circular shape is often the easiest and the sturdiest way to set it up. You can also purchase wire bins that are made from galvanized metal mesh. They come in several shapes and sizes and are easy to set up.

PLASTIC-BIN COMPOSTING

You'll find many different types of plastic compost bins on the market. Plastic bins are easier to move around, last longer than wooden bins, and protect your compost from the rain and sun. They come in round or square shapes; some have solid sides, and others have removable and stackable sides. Most have a capacity of 12 cubic feet, which is the size needed for your compost to heat up, but you can also find larger bins.

TUMBLER COMPOSTING

Another option is to purchase a compost tumbler. Tumblers are convenient because every time you rotate the drum, you turn the material, which will make it decompose faster. However, compost material can become very heavy and it can be difficult to turn the barrel when it is full. Tumblers can also keep the material too wet, so you need to be aware of how much moisture you are adding to the bin.

WHAT TO COMPOST

There are a few key components to a healthy compost pile, primarily using materials that will decompose and are safe to enter the food system, and creating a balance of the different materials you use. Using compost is also an important part of organic gardening, and focusing on soil health will help you to create compost that is highly nutritious.

First, and most important, the materials that comprise your compost pile need to be able to decompose. Common kitchen waste—vegetable remains and coffee grounds as well as other household and garden items such as wood, paper, and plant material—are commonly composted materials. Remember that when you add your finished compost to your garden soil, the decomposed materials in the compost will become a part of the system that produces your food, so it is very important that the compost be made up of safe materials. The easiest way to do this is to focus on using organic materials that will add health to your garden and the food that you grow.

The next step to a healthy compost pile is to create a mixture of different types of materials. Creating the right mixture will keep your compost pile healthy and free of strong odor. A properly balanced compost pile will have a mixture of green material, brown material, and manures or good soil. Too much green material will attract flies and give your compost a strong odor, and too much brown material will slow down the decomposition of the pile.

The green material adds nitrogen to your pile. Some common green-material items you can use are vegetable kitchen waste, animal or human hair, weeds that have not gone to seed, green garden debris, cut grass, and seaweed.

The brown material adds carbon to your pile. Some common brown materials are thick vegetable stems such as those from broccoli and cornstalks, coffee grounds, shredded dried leaves, small wood shavings, straw, hay, twigs, wood ashes, and sawdust.

Depending on where you live, many of these items might be easily found at home, but if you do not have enough material to get started, check out your neighborhood for items you can use. Do your neighbors have leaves you can rake up and use? Do they use their grass clippings? Be careful not to use grass clippings where pesticides have been added! If you live near a beach, go foraging for seaweed. Coffee grounds are a great addition to a compost pile and often coffee shops will give coffee grounds away for free—but remember that unless they are organic, coffee grounds are often laced with pesticides. Accumulate these items and then build your pile all at once.

Smaller materials will break down more quickly, so avoid putting large pieces of wood or cardboard into the pile. Shred large twigs, leaves, cornstalks, and broccoli stalks first or they will take a long time to decompose. Using a variety of materials with different textures will give your pile better air circulation, which will make better compost. A pile with only one or two materials in it will take longer to decompose.

There are certain materials that should never be put in your compost pile because they will not decompose or they may carry diseases that you do not want in the final product. Do *not* include any of the following items in your compost: dog, cat, or human feces; animal urine; large amounts of oil; pine needles; meat products or bones; oak leaves; toxic materials; or materials treated with pesticides.

It is not usually necessary to add organic fertilizers to your compost because the green and brown matter will make rich compost on its own. But if you know your soil is deficient in a certain element or elements, then by all means add a little to your compost pile. Organic fertilizers such as rock powder, blood meal, bone meal, cottonseed meal, kelp, greensand, and peat moss can be used to increase the nutrient level and to correct the pH if necessary. Simply add a handful of any of these in between your green and brown layers. You can also add lime to neutralize the acidity in your compost. Dolomite lime is the best form to add because it has a combination of calcium and magnesium in it. Any garden center will carry a variety of soil amendments meant to adjust and correct the pH of your soil.

SEEDS AND PLANTING

In order to have the best veggies on hand when whipping up the recipes in the following chapters, you will want to know how to set your vegetables up for success from seeds and how to troubleshoot any issues that may arise during the growing process.

BUY OR SAVE?

To grow healthy vegetable plants, you need to start with healthy seeds and transplants. Buy your seeds from a reputable seller or—even better—save your own seeds, especially if you find a certain variety that does well in your garden. A reputable seller should be willing to answer all of your questions, provide you with information on where and how the seeds were grown, and give you growing tips. If your garden site is susceptible to certain pests or diseases, try to find seed varieties that are resistant to those problems. Seed catalogs have valuable information regarding different varieties of seeds. Choosing the right varieties of vegetable plants for your garden will help keep the soil and plants healthier.

GROW.

Visiting local nurseries or garden centers that start their own plants from seed is often a safer way to purchase pest-free seedlings. Additionally, these seedlings have been grown in a climate and region that battles the very same pests and diseases that your own garden is susceptible to. Buying seedlings locally will give your garden a healthy head start and also allows you to take advantage of the experience of local growers in your area.

The plants that produce the first fruits or pods are the plants you want to mark for seed saving. This is often difficult to do, as most gardeners cannot wait to harvest the first tasty produce of the season. Tie a ribbon in an obvious location on the plant you want to mark for saving seed so you'll be reminded not to harvest this plant. Simply remove the seeds from the plant when ready and store them out of reach of sunlight.

When you purchase plants or transplants, make sure they are healthy. Many gardeners have unknowingly brought pests and diseases into their gardens via transplants. Look closely at any transplants you plan to bring home. Check for any insects in the soil or on the undersides of the leaves, holes in the leaves, and evidence that insects have chewed the leaves. These are all signs that the plant may be infested. Make sure the plant looks healthy. The stem should be strong and thick, the leaves should be well-formed and bright green, and the plant should not be root bound.

STARTING YOUR OWN SEEDS, INDOORS AND OUTDOORS

There are two ways to plant your vegetable seeds: directly outdoors into the soil or indoors in seed trays to be transplanted to the garden later. Different vegetable seeds have different requirements for germination and maturing; some need heat and some do better in cool weather. You must know the best way to start each of your vegetables. Most vegetable seeds will do well either way, but some vegetables, such as root crops, need to be seeded directly because they do not grow well if their roots are disturbed.

Vegetables best started by seeding directly into the soil include beans, beets, carrots, corn, garlic, peas, potatoes, radish, rutabagas, and salad greens.

Some vegetables are difficult to start outdoors because the seed needs a very specific temperature to germinate. These are best started indoors so you have more control over their growing conditions. Some examples are tomatoes, peppers, and eggplants.

GROW.

Most homes have at least one window that gets enough sunlight to start a tray of seedlings, but depending on your climate, the amount and strength of sunlight might be a little too weak to give your seedlings the light and warmth that they need to start off strong. If your plants start to look long and spindly and not very robust, this means that the climate is not warm and sunny enough. By incorporating a few grow lights, or sometimes just a space heater, you can adjust your indoor climate to be warm and "sunny" enough to start successful seedlings at home.

TRELLISING AND STAKING

Some vegetable plants need support to grow and produce healthy fruits or pods. Tomatoes and cucumbers do best if they can grow upright so that the fruit is not lying on the ground and the plant can receive both light and air circulation. Some varieties of peas and beans can grow up to 6 feet high or more and need support, and many of the small fruit plants described in Chapter 4 require trellising. These climbing plants have vines that need to be able to attach to a structure of some sort in order to continue to grow taller. Some common vine and sprawling vegetables include climbing and runner beans, cucumbers, snow and snap peas, summer squash, and tomatoes.

It is important to know which plants will need staking or a trellis so that you can put these up just before you plant the seeds or set out your transplants. If you wait, you can disturb the roots, which can cause stress, and the vines of different plants can grow into each other, making it difficult to place a stake or trellis without damaging the plants.

Growing vertically can save a lot of space, especially if you have a tiny garden site or grow in containers on your balcony. The plants are often healthier because they don't touch the wet or cold ground, and therefore attract fewer pests and diseases. Mildew and rot are common problems for many fruiting vegetables, so it's to your advantage to keep the fruit off the ground. When your plants grow upright, you can easily see the fruit to harvest. Gardening can be backbreaking work, and harvesting off an upright structure can alleviate some of this stress on your body.

Trellis and staking material can be purchased at most garden centers or from seed catalogs. You can also make structures of your own out of materials you have on hand. Plastic or nylon netting, wooden frames, wire cages, wooden stakes, or teepee structures are common types of trellises and stakes. With a little experimentation and ingenuity, most can be adapted to your garden's specific needs. When choosing methods to use, the most resourceful thing you can do is to adapt materials you already have on hand to meet your needs.

COMPANION PLANTING

Companion planting is a common method used by gardeners, especially space-conscious gardeners in suburban and urban areas. The basic idea of companion planting is to utilize the complementary components of different plants to create a system where crops are working together with less outside support to meet their needs. The classic example of companion planting is a system called the Three Sisters.

The Three Sisters system includes three crops: squash, corn, and beans. This system has deep historical roots and is famously tied to stories of Native

Americans teaching this system to European settlers. The plants that are employed comprise a traditional North American staple diet, because in addition to their complementary growing characteristics, their nutritional components complement each other well. There are different ways to employ the Three Sisters, but the general concept is that the cornstalk acts as a climbing support for the beans, the beans provide nitrogen to the soil, and the foliage of the squash acts as a cover to block out weeds. The best way to plant the Three Sisters is by using a mound system that alternates crops, and to pay attention to seed spacing, timing of plantings, and water drainage and absorption. You will also want to choose seed varieties that suit one another well.

Companion planting can also be used as part of an integrated pest management plan by finding a balance between the contributions of different plants and using crops as allies for one another. As you become more and more familiar with the different crops that you grow, you will understand what each one gives and takes, and can plant accordingly.

MAINTENANCE AND UPKEEP: WATERING, WEEDING, PEST AND DISEASE CONTROL

One of the most rewarding parts of gardening is learning to apply the creative and critical thinking that is needed to problem-solve issues. Gardening is not an exact science, and each season there will be new problems and new solutions to try out. Don't let this scare you. Learning how to adapt your system as you go is exciting and fun. Half the fun in planning your garden during the winter is trying to figure out how to make everything run smoother than it did the year before.

WATERING: TOO MUCH OR TOO LITTLE?

Your crops need water to grow, mature, and produce fruits, pods, or seeds for you to enjoy. The amount of water each plant requires depends on your climate, your soil, and the type of fruit or vegetable. All these variables make watering a complex subject. When you assessed your site, you began the process of deciding what type of watering system would work best for you. In this section you will learn what underwatering and overwatering can look like. By applying this knowledge to the watering systems described in Chapter 1, you can adapt your watering systems as necessary.

Signs of Underwatering

A plant's roots must continually grow for the plant to stay healthy and produce its fruit, seeds, or buds. The roots draw the nutrients from the soil up into the plant to make it grow. Water allows the nutrients in the soil to be absorbed into the plant. If there is too little water, the roots cannot draw in the nutrients. As a result, the plant will not grow and mature as it should. You can water the surface or even the top several inches of your soil, but the plant roots need to go deeper into the soil to get more nutrients. This is why it is essential for regular deep watering when growing vegetables.

Wilted plants are one sign that you're not watering enough. If the plant can draw enough water to replace the amount that is evaporated from its leaves, it will remain upright and strong. If the plant is not getting the water it needs, it will quickly collapse. This causes severe stress to the plant and often death. It is important to water a plant that is wilted as soon as you can. Take time every day to observe your plants so you can find and quickly fix potential problems. Your plants should appear strong, have a bright color, and look healthy. If you have young transplants, you need to give them a drink of water every day because their roots are very shallow and the top few inches of your soil can dry out very quickly. Too little water can lead to poor root development, which will make for an unhealthy plant.

Once your vegetable plants have begun to mature, watering them once a week is usually sufficient. For some plants, it is best to stop watering them altogether once they have matured. For example, onions and potatoes need less water as they get close to maturity.

If you notice any of the following signs in your plants, chances are they are not getting enough water:

- The plants appear small and are very slow growing.
- The plants are not producing very many fruits, seeds, or buds, and the ones being produced are often misshapen.
- The plants are diseased.
- The plants are yellowish or pale in color, or the plants are wilting. (Some natural wilting may occur in the heat of the day, but if your plants do not perk up by late afternoon, you do have a problem.)

Signs of Overwatering

Most gardeners go to great lengths to make sure they add enough nutrients to their garden beds. When the soil is moist, the water helps hold the nutrients to rock particles in the soil so the plant roots can absorb them. If there is too much water in the soil, a process called leaching occurs. The excess water drains lower into the soil and takes a lot of the nutrients with it. Vegetable plant roots grow to different depths, but most do not grow below 2½ feet. If the excess water has washed away the nutrients, there is less nourishment available for the roots to absorb. Without proper food, the plant will not grow and mature as you may expect it to.

Plants also need good air circulation to breathe. If the soil is saturated with water, there isn't any room left in the soil for air circulation. If the air supply is cut off for any length of time, the plant roots will rot, killing the plant. That's why it's crucial to know your own soil conditions. Keep a record of rainfall and regularly check the moisture in your soil either with a moisture meter or by digging into the soil with your hands or a small shovel to see how far down the moisture is. Water when needed. If you are a novice gardener, it can take time to get to know your soil and climate, so initially it is important to observe and jot down some notes to refer back to the following season.

Combating Drainage Problems

You need fertile, well-drained soil to grow great vegetables; however, most gardeners are not blessed with perfect soil or the perfect garden site.

How do you make your soil healthier and get proper drainage if you live in a rainy climate or if you have soggy soil? What do you do if you have the opposite problem—a sandy soil that does not hold any amount of water? How do you increase the amount of moisture in this type of soil?

Adding organic material is the solution to both problems. It will help lighten heavy soil so the water can drain better, and it will add more organic material to sandy soil to help hold the water in. Aged animal manure, compost, or well-drained topsoil will help. Add in as much as possible—several inches if you can get enough. It is important to add in organic matter every year because you inevitably lose soil through erosion and the process of harvesting your plants. Mulching—covering the soil around plants with organic material—is another way to protect your soil from being blown away or nutrients from being leached out. Using cover crops to hold in nutrients and prevent erosion is another important way to maintain your soil.

If you have an extreme problem with drainage, call a landscaper or other expert to assess the situation for you. Underground drainage pipes can help remove any excess water you may have in your garden site. Well-drained soil helps keep the plant roots from becoming waterlogged, allowing them to absorb the nutrients and oxygen needed to grow and mature. Poorly drained soil leaves your vegetable plants more susceptible to root rot and soil-borne diseases, so get help with drainage if this is a problem in your garden site.

CONTROLLING WEEDS

A weed is just a plant that grows where it is not wanted. This means that weeds will sometimes be vegetable plants that are growing where you did not intend them to be. You may find that a carrot plant, or some other misplaced veggie, snuck into a bed of greens. It's hard not to admire the determination of these plants, but in order to keep your garden organized and growing according to plan, you still need to remove these weeds.

It is important to keep your garden beds weeded when your vegetable plants are small so your plants get a good start. Weeds compete for the nutrients in the soil, often taking over and leaving your veggie plants without the valuable food they need to grow and mature. In this section you will learn different techniques to help keep your garden weed-free—or at least to help you keep weeds under control.

Know Your Weeds

Weed seeds are introduced to your garden by birds, the wind, and the bottoms of your shoes. If a soil will not support weeds, it will not support your vegetables, so weeds are a sign that your soil is fertile. Seeds are brought to the surface by digging or tilling the soil. Once they are exposed to the light, they start growing. Some weeds can grow very fast, stealing the light, nutrients, and space from your vegetable plants.

There are three types of weeds: annuals, biennials, and perennials. Annual weeds live for only one season, but they produce thousands of seeds to ensure their survival. They germinate in the spring, produce seeds in the summer, and die in the fall. The best way to control annual weeds is to pull them out or cut them off with a hoe before they go to seed. Annual weeds grow quickly, so you need to stay on top of these so they do not spread their seed. Some examples of common annual weeds are knotweed, pigweed, purslane, lamb's quarters, and chickweed.

A biennial weed grows the first year but does not produce flowers or seeds until the second year of growth. The best way to control these weeds is to remove them from your garden in the first year of their growth so they have no chance of spreading their seeds. Common biennial weeds include burdock, mullein, and Queen Anne's lace.

Perennial weeds live for years. Some produce seeds and others spread via their roots or bulbs. Perennial weeds often have deep roots that creep underground, making them difficult to eradicate. To control them, you should dig them out, removing as much of the root as you can. You often have to pull these weeds on a regular basis in order to get all of the root system. Some common perennial weeds are dandelion, thistle, bindweed, chicory, plantain, wild sorrel, and dock.

Woody perennials include poison ivy, kudzu, some types of morning glory (which is a type of bindweed), and Japanese honeysuckle. These are often invasive and are spread mainly by birds that love the seeds of these plants. Some of these plants need only a piece of stem to come in contact with soil to begin growing, so they can multiply quickly.

Grasses are another invasive perennial weed. They can make some of the worst weeds because they produce a lot of seeds and the plants are difficult to uproot. Quackgrass and some varieties of bamboo are common grasses that are considered weeds, especially in the vegetable garden. These plants produce underground roots and stems, and new plants pop up several yards away from the parent plant, making them difficult to remove.

What Weeds Can Tell You

You can learn a great deal about your soil by observing the weeds that grow in your garden. They can point to soil imbalances such as poor drainage, lack of water, low fertility, lack of aeration, and nutrient deficiency. Certain weeds only grow in poor soil, which gives you an indication that you need to add more amendments and fertilize your garden area if you want to grow a successful vegetable garden. Correcting the imbalances in your soil often means you will be able to eradicate certain weeds. Taking time to observe what weeds are growing in your garden area can be especially important if you are planning to start a new garden in a certain area, or if you are looking for some property to purchase with the intention of growing your own food or growing to sell.

Weed Your Garden

Spring brings new growth to your vegetable garden. The seeds begin to sprout and the transplants start to grow—and so do the weeds. Spring is the time to pay attention to your weeds. Weeds often grow faster than your vegetable plants, so weeds can overtake vegetable plants and steal the sunlight and nutrients your veggie plants need. It is easier to kill the weeds when they are small and the soil is moist rather than later when the soil is hard and dry. Always remove the weeds before they go to seed.

Getting on your hands and knees and pulling weeds (getting the roots if you can) is probably the best way to get rid of weeds in your vegetable garden. This can be time-consuming, but if you set aside time each week to do a patch, you will be pleasantly surprised that it can be easy to stay ahead of weeds. You can also use a hoe to speed up the process. You cannot always replace the thoroughness of hand weeding by using tools, but you can find an efficient and thorough balance.

Mulch

After weeding your garden bed, add mulch to the area. Weed seeds need light to germinate and grow, so the main function of mulch in weed control is to prevent light from reaching the seeds. Cover the area completely with up to 4 inches of mulch, leaving a few inches clear around the base of the plant stem. You'll often have mulch materials handy from your own garden. Two common materials are leaves and grass. Raking leaves and then running the lawn mower over them to shred them makes great mulch. Collecting your grass clippings in a mower bag is another mulch that costs no money and is easy to get. Just make sure you do not use pesticides on your lawn; you do not want to contaminate your vegetable patch. Keep in mind that you can create a mulching system that combats weeds and assists with season extension.

Mulch also has its disadvantages, however. Mulch can promote fungus and disease, especially if it keeps the soil too damp and cold. Slugs and mice love mulch, so use mulches sparingly if you live in an area where these are a problem. Using certain types of mulch can cause deficiencies in your soil. For example, pine needles are very acidic and may make it more difficult to grow vegetables in a soil that is already acidic. Sawdust uses up nitrogen to decompose, which it does at the expense of your plants. It is important to understand what materials are best for your garden site and the reasons why you are using mulch.

Other Ways to Control Weeds

One great way to prevent weeds is not to bring them into your garden. Keep any tools you work with clean. Remove any weeds that have gone to seed from your garden. When shopping for plants, make sure there are no weeds in the containers. When you bring in hay or straw to your garden, make sure it comes from a weed-free source. If it is not weed-free, you may soon find hay growing in your garden beds. Animal manures can have lots of weed seeds in them, so make sure you know what kind of bedding was used and what the animals were fed. All of these small things can make it easier to keep your garden free of weeds, or at least to make sure you are not introducing new weeds to the area.

Growing a cover crop can smother weeds. By adding a cover crop you can enrich your soil as well as control weeds. Cultivate or dig the area and then sow the green manure thickly. Turn the green manure over before the weeds you are trying to control have a chance to set seed. To be most effective, you will need to grow and turn two or three cover crops in succession. By growing vegetables close together, you can reduce the number of weeds by shading them from the sun. Grow your lettuces close together so they overlap each other, or grow your squash under your corn to prevent weeds from getting any light.

Weeds Can Be Good

Weeds do have some benefits to your garden as well. Many perennial weeds are deep-rooted, which helps bring nutrients to the surface so your vegetable plants have access to them. The deep roots also aerate the soil, which can be helpful, especially if you have drainage problems in your garden site. Weeds will grow when most other plants will not and are beneficial for preventing soil erosion and leaching of nutrients due to heavy rainfall. Many weeds are a great food source for bees, butterflies, birds, and beneficial insects, which all help control unwanted pests and diseases in your vegetable garden.

Weeds can be composted as long as they have been pulled before they go to seed. If you have only pulled a few weeds, you can leave them to dry in your pathway; however, if you have a whole bucketful of weeds, it is best to remove them from the garden, because they can attract pests. Place them into your compost instead; they are a good source of green matter.

Most gardeners consider comfrey and stinging nettle to be weeds, but these herbs can be added to your compost or used to make a nitrogen-rich fertilizer tea. Both of these plants draw up and store nitrogen in their leaves. When they are composted or made into teas, the nitrogen is released.

There are many edible weeds that you can harvest to use in cooking. Stinging nettle, dandelion greens, purslane, lamb's quarter, and burdock are all edible (and actually fetch high prices at some high-end farmers' markets). Comfrey and stinging nettle also are used in teas and healing salves. It is important to do the research and know exactly what plant you are harvesting before you ingest it. However, once you know what weeds are edible or offer health benefits, you will have a whole new outlook and even more choices to add to your dinner table—and the weeds grew without any work on your part!

PESTS AND DISEASES

No garden is without pests and diseases, but the important thing is to control them before they become a problem. The secret is taking the time to observe your garden. You can keep your plants healthy by using natural controls and promoting beneficial insects.

Natural Animal and Pest Control

There are some easy ways to control any animal or pest problems you may still have, even if you are adhering to all the practices outlined in this chapter. It is important to observe your garden on a regular basis so you can catch any potential problems early on; problems are much easier to handle if only a few plants are infected.

Larger pests or animals can cause a lot of damage in vegetable gardens. Deer, elk, raccoons, squirrels, opossum, skunks, gophers, and bears like vegetables just as much as we do. Take the time to observe what kind of animal is entering your garden. They often come out and feed at dusk or dawn. If it's not a wild animal, maybe your neighbor's dog or cat is sneaking in and digging up your plants. Keep watch to see what is causing the problem.

Helpful or Harmful?

It takes time to get to know what is living in or entering your garden, and each year may bring a new problem. Learn by asking fellow gardeners, reading books, checking on the Internet, or asking questions at your local nursery or garden center. Check your local library, community education center, or food cooperative to learn about gardening classes offered in your area.

Vegetable gardening is a new experience each season because you cannot predict what will happen. Do not be afraid to experiment with new plant varieties and try out different natural controls. Stay away from pesticides when it comes to your vegetable garden; they will not make your soil healthier and will kill the beneficial insects as well as the pests. Pesticides in insects may also harm birds and other animals that feed on these insects. Attracting and keeping beneficial animals and insects in your garden brings you closer to having healthier plants and a more abundant vegetable harvest.

Birds, bats, toads, and snakes are all creatures you want in your garden. They will keep slugs, snails, and many insects under control. You help attract wanted creatures by adding habitats and feeders, like bird houses, and water sources like bird baths and garden fountains, to your outdoor space.

Common Diseases

You may physically see a pest or insect, but it is more difficult to diagnose a plant disease because the symptoms can be similar to those caused by other factors such as excessive heat or cold, nutrient deficiencies in the soil, or poor drainage. Having healthy soil, giving your plants proper water and fertilizer, and maintaining good garden practices minimizes your plants' vulnerability to many diseases. If you do have a recurring problem, it is important to learn what it is and to try to correct the cause.

There are four main types of pathogens that cause disease in vegetable plants: bacteria, fungi, nematodes (roundworms), and viruses. They all attack plants in different ways but produce some common symptoms in plants such as wilting, yellowing, and stunted growth. The pathogens can be spread in various ways. They can be blown around by the wind or carried in water. Animals, humans, garden tools, and other equipment can also transfer pathogens from plant to plant. Insects can carry a pathogen in their saliva and transfer it from plant to plant. When you are trying to diagnose a disease, it is important to learn the life cycle of the pathogen so you can avoid spreading it.

For a disease to occur, three elements must be present in your garden: a susceptible plant, a pathogen, and favorable conditions for the pathogen to survive. To control or manage plant diseases, you need to remove one or more of these elements. A disease cannot develop if one of these elements is missing. Pulling out and destroying the infected vegetable plant removes the pathogen. You can also make it difficult for pathogens to survive by creating an environment that is not compatible for them. For example, avoid overhead watering, or trellis a plant so it has better air circulation. Both measures make it more difficult for the pathogen to survive.

The best way to keep your vegetable garden free of pests and diseases is to have healthy soil, give your plants the proper amount of water, practice crop rotation, and keep your garden and tools clean. A healthy plant will be better able to fight off anything that comes its way. No vegetable garden will be totally free of all pests or diseases, and remember that you want beneficial insects and animals to stay around.

READY TO GO?

Now that you know how to troubleshoot any issues that may arise in your garden—and how to keep problems from happening in the first place—are you ready to get your hands dirty? Read on!

PART 2

GROW AND COOK

CHAPTER 3

VEGETABLES

For the self-sufficient gardener, vegetables are the most significant crop to grow. In Chapter 1, you started thinking about what you could grow in your garden space and what you and your family like to eat. In this chapter you'll learn about the individual needs of the specific vegetable plants you have chosen to grow. For example, some vegetable plants grow best upright or vertical; others like to be protected from the hot sun, wind, or rain. All of these factors need to be considered when planning your vegetable garden layout. In addition, you'll find a variety of delicious, fresh, farm-to-table recipes that will teach you how to cook your garden's bounty. Enjoy!

BEANS, PEAS, AND PERENNIAL VEGETABLES

Freshly picked beans and peas are two of the tastiest treats from the garden. They are easy to grow in pots or raised beds, can be trellised to add structure to your garden, and have lovely flowers that enhance your vegetable garden's appearance. The other vegetables that will be discussed in this section—artichokes, asparagus, and sun chokes—are all perennial veggies; they die back in the fall and emerge again in the spring.

BEANS

Beans are one of the easiest vegetables to grow. You sow the seeds directly into the garden, where they will germinate quickly in the right temperature and grow vigorously. Considering the small amount of space they take up in your garden, beans produce an awfully plentiful bounty. There are several different types of beans—bush beans (sometimes called snap beans), runner beans, pole beans, shelling beans for drying, lima beans, soybeans, and fava beans (sometimes called broad beans). Most varieties need warm soil to germinate, so they are usually planted in late spring. To tell whether it's time to plant your beans, walk barefoot on the soil at midday. If the soil feels cold, hold off for a while; if it doesn't feel cold, you're ready to plant. The exception to this is fava beans, which are a cool-weather bean and best planted in early spring.

Beans grow at various heights. Bush beans grow to a height of 16 inches; on the other end of the spectrum, pole and runner beans can grow up to 8 feet tall. The type of beans you want to grow will determine whether they need support.

As we discussed, beans will grow in almost any reasonably good garden soil, but grow best in a sandy, loamy soil with a neutral pH. Beans do not like a lot of moisture before they germinate, but they need regular watering once they have sprouted in order to produce tender beans. They are best harvested young and need to be picked every few days so the plant knows that it needs to keep producing more beans.

Fresh beans won't last for much more than a week in your refrigerator, but they can be stored easily either by drying (preferred) or by canning or freezing. To freeze beans you will first need to blanch them (plunge them into boiling water for a short time) and they'll only keep for several months in the freezer versus the several years they can keep if they are harvested and dried properly. Beans that you buy from the grocery in bags are dried beans (versus canned beans that are also common in stores).

To cook dried beans, you will need to first soak them overnight. After the beans have been soaked, you can slowly cook them over a span of several hours, adding a little oil (I prefer canola because its neutral flavor doesn't take away from the beans' flavor), salt, pepper, garlic, onion, and any other seasoning that you prefer. The beans should be cooked at a low heat and stirred occasionally to prevent burning or sticking. If you have a pressure cooker, you can achieve similar results to slow-cooking in about forty minutes.

COOK.

Cooking beans in a pressure cooker is one of the best ways to enjoy dried beans without the hassle of soaking and slow-cooking them. To achieve success with beans in your pressure cooker, follow the chart that came with your specific pressure cooker for water-to-bean ratio. It is best to bring the water to a boil before adding the beans. The trick to cooking unsoaked beans in a pressure cooker is to add a spoonful of oil to the water. This decreases the amount of foam that is produced, making it less likely to clog the pressure vent.

PEAS

Peas are a cool-weather vegetable; they do best when planted in the early spring. If you live in a climate that has mild winters, do a second planting in mid-August for a fall harvest. Peas can withstand a little frost. They like a rich, well-drained soil that is not too high in nitrogen. They like organic matter, so mix in several inches of compost or aged animal manure when preparing the garden bed.

There are three different types of peas. Shelling peas are grown for the seeds. Snow peas have a flat, edible pod and are often used in stir-fries. Snap peas have an edible pod and seeds that are eaten together. There are several varieties of each of these types of peas. Some peas will need to be staked; snow peas and snap peas can grow up to 5 feet high.

Peas need moisture to germinate, and they often germinate faster if the seed is first soaked overnight. Because peas are planted in the spring, it is important that the seed and plants do not get waterlogged or they will most likely rot. Peas are best stored frozen and can keep for several months in a freezer. They can also be dried and canned.

ARTICHOKES

The globe artichoke is easy to grow, is relatively disease-free, and can make a stunning addition to any garden. It grows rapidly and can grow up to 6 feet tall and just as wide. It is a cool-season perennial vegetable that will grow vigorously and produce for four to five years. Just a few plants will produce enough artichokes for a small family.

The globe artichoke is known as an exotic plant, and it's not a common vegetable for most home gardeners. However, it is definitely worth growing, especially if you are looking to plant something new. This stately plant has gray-green leaves and produces flower buds that resemble elongated pinecones. The cones are green and layered with edible bracts, but the heart of the cone is the true delicacy. If the plant is left to mature, a large bud opens to reveal a purple thistle flower. This flower can be dried and is often used in floral arrangements.

Globe artichokes will produce some buds the first year, but they are best harvested in the second or third year after planting when they are producing between twelve and thirty buds on each plant. This is also about the time when they are becoming crowded and need to be divided. They require a cool period before they can flower but are sensitive to the cold and may be grown only as annuals if you live in a cold northern climate. Even if you live in a milder climate, it is best to cut the plants back to about 6 inches above the ground and protect the roots from freezing by using thick mulch.

SUN CHOKES

Sun chokes, often known as Jerusalem artichokes, are not related to the globe artichoke in any way. The "Jerusalem" tag came from a misunderstanding of the Italian word *girasole*, meaning "sunflower." The term *artichoke* comes from an Arabic word meaning "thistle," which relates to the plant's appearance. It is a perennial vegetable that belongs to the sunflower family. The underground tuber is the part that is harvested and eaten.

Sun chokes will grow in any kind of soil and they often grow quickly and prolifically. Plant tubers in the spring, giving them a large area to grow (they can grow up to 6 feet tall). They produce yellow flowers a little smaller in size than the common sunflower. When the leaves die back in the fall, the tubers can be harvested. They will winter over in the ground and will taste sweeter after a frost. Sun chokes are a low-calorie alternative to potatoes.

ASPARAGUS

Asparagus is another perennial vegetable. Plant it in a permanent area; once planted, it will produce new shoots each spring and will do so for fifteen to twenty years without too much work on your part. It is best to buy one-year-old crowns, or rhizomes, as they take three years to grow from seed to harvest. In the first year of planting, resist cutting any of the spears so they can leaf out. The feathery foliage will nourish the roots, which in turn will give you more spears in the second year. In the second year, you can harvest the first few spears, but stop harvesting once the spears start to look spindly or have a diameter less than ¼ inch. In the third and following years, you will be able to harvest over a much longer season.

When preparing an asparagus bed, dig in generous amounts of compost or aged animal manure. This can be done by digging a trench a foot deep in your bed and then filling it with 3 to 4 inches of organic material. Mix this with the existing soil. Lay the crowns in the trench and cover them with 2 inches of soil, but do not cover the tips of the shoots. As the plant grows, you can add more soil around the plant.

In the fall, cut back the fernlike foliage of the asparagus plant. This is also a great time to mulch the bed with aged animal manure to add nutrients to the soil as it decomposes over the winter. Leaves or straw can be added on top for more protection from the cold, but avoid mulching with sawdust, which is often too acidic for the plant.

ROOT VEGGIES

Root vegetables are grown for their edible roots. The veggies in this section are all easy to grow and have similar growing needs and soil conditions. Root veggies need a well-prepared garden bed with a light soil to grow their best. Here you'll find easy tips on how to grow some common root vegetables including beets, carrots, potatoes, radishes, and rutabagas. We will also discuss growing garlic, leeks, and onions, which are grown mainly for their roots but have some distinctive characteristics of their own.

BEETS

Beets are a love-or-hate vegetable; either you love them or you have no desire to eat them at all. They are a great addition to any home garden because they are easy to grow, have a long harvest, take up a small amount of space in your garden, and can be stored. They have more than one edible part and can be eaten raw or cooked, so they are a very versatile vegetable. The young leaves are used with other baby greens in popular salad mixes. The mature leaves, beet greens, can be steamed for a nutritious side dish to add to any meal. The roots can be harvested as sweet and tender baby beets, or they can be left to grow to maturity to be harvested as you need them all summer and fall.

The many varieties of beets give you more options than just a round red beet. You can buy seeds that will produce elongated roots, which have a milder taste. Beets can now be grown in a multitude of colors. There are white, yellow, orange, and striped varieties. Beets like a fairly rich soil that is free of rocks and debris. Add in aged animal manure and lime if needed when preparing your garden bed. Make sure your bed is well prepared with at least a foot of loose tilled soil for the roots to grow. Remove any lumps, rocks, or sticks from the soil so they don't impede the growth of the root.

Beets are usually direct-seeded to your garden bed; however, they are slow to germinate, so mark the bed where they are planted. The seed can produce more than one plant. They will need to be thinned so there is only one plant for every 3 to 4 inches of garden soil as the seedlings start to grow. To store beets you can pickle them, can them, or keep them in a root cellar.

CARROTS

Carrots are one of the most popular vegetables in the world. Pulling a carrot from the garden, wiping off a little dirt, and biting into it is an experience everyone should have. There is nothing better than a tender, freshly picked carrot! Carrots are great to grow if you have children around because carrots grow fairly quickly and can be picked at any size—and children love to pull them out of the ground.

The time-consuming part of growing carrots is the bed preparation. In order to grow their best, carrots need a deep, loose sandy soil that is free of debris. They are a great vegetable to grow in raised beds because the soil texture is often lighter than in a regular garden bed. If you have a heavy soil, it is important to dig in compost or aged animal manure to lighten the soil. However, if the soil is too fertile, the carrots may get hairy and misshapen, and may not taste as good. It can take a few years to get your soil to the proper consistency to grow fabulous carrots. If there are any obstructions in the soil, the carrot will grow around them, producing oddly shaped roots. So before planting your carrot seeds it is important to take the time to break up any lumps of soil and pick out rocks that are larger than very small pebbles.

Carrots are a cool-season crop and are best planted in early spring to be harvested in the summer. If you live in an area with mild winters, plant another crop in late summer for a fall harvest. The carrot has its best flavor when grown in the full sun with cool nights. Carrots are direct-seeded and need to be kept moist in order to germinate, so you may have to water the garden bed two to three times a day until they germinate. Water carefully so as not to wash the seeds away. It is important to keep the soil moistened because the seeds may not be able to break through hard and crusty soil if the soil dries out.

To harvest large carrots so they do not break off, gently push the carrot downward into the ground and then pull it upward. This breaks the roots and makes the carrot easier to pull up.

When storing carrots, you need to remove the green, leafy tops. This is true whether you are storing them in your fridge (where they will keep in a sealed plastic bag for several weeks or more), freezing them (blanch them first), canning them (you will need to use a pressure cooker), or storing them in your root cellar (carrots buried in sand and stored in a root cellar will keep for several months). If you want to store a large amount of carrots, or more than you have indoor space for, you can leave them in the ground covered with several inches of mulch and harvest as you need them, although they will become less sweet and will lose their tenderness the longer they are in the ground.

POTATOES

Potatoes are the most-used vegetable in the world. They are nutritious, versatile, easy to grow, and ideal for storage. Potatoes are closely related to tomatoes; like tomato plants, potatoes produce sprawling and bushy vines above ground. However, potatoes produce tubers underground. They need a long growing season—approximately four months with continuous cool weather for best production. When preparing your potato bed, make sure the soil is well tilled with compost or aged animal manure added to it. Potatoes need a more acidic soil, so never lime the area where they will be planted.

Plant potatoes as early as you can get into your garden. They are grown from stem cuttings, which are also called seed pieces, or seed eyes. When planting, you can cut the seed potato into pieces; just make sure each section has at least three eyes. The potato plant can take up a lot of room, and several plants will be needed for a small family to eat fresh potatoes. You'll want even more plants if you want to store potatoes for use during the winter months.

The potato seed does not need much water until it has sprouted above ground. After the vine starts to grow, keep mounding soil up against the new growth; this is called *hilling*. This allows the tuber to grow without being exposed to the sun; too much sun exposure will cause the potato to turn green. You can harvest young potatoes after the plant has flowered by digging around the base of the plant with your hands. The tubers are mature and ready to be harvested once the vine has turned brown and died back. Potatoes are excellent for storing and will keep for several months if stored properly. Make sure they are dry before storing them in a cool, dark area.

GROW.

Potatoes are a nutrient-rich vegetable and comprise the majority of many native diets. By growing lots of different varieties of potatoes and storing them throughout the winter, you and your family will have most of the nutrition that you need to stay healthy. Did you know that the only essential nutrient potatoes lack is vitamin D? When cooked with milk, as in mashed potatoes, potatoes make a perfect superfood.

RUTABAGAS AND TURNIPS

The rutabaga and turnip are closely related cousins. Both are cool-season crops and both like fertile, well-drained soil that is well tilled so the roots have a lot of space to grow. The young greens make a great addition to a salad mix or can be steamed as a healthy green vegetable. They are filled with calcium and other nutrients. The roots from both vegetables can be eaten raw but are most often cooked in soups or stews or mashed as a side dish.

The rutabaga is a hardy, slow-growing root vegetable that is normally planted in early to midsummer and then harvested in the fall. It has large, yellow roots and is often called a winter turnip or swede. The young leaves can be eaten, but they get coarse once they mature. Rutabagas are hardy enough to remain in the garden all winter and can be harvested as you need them. They need a fair amount of space because the roots can grow quite large, weighing 2 to 3 pounds each.

The turnip has a small, white, round root with a purple skin. It grows like a large radish. The greens can be eaten young or as mature leaves; turnips are sometime grown just for the leaves. Turnip seeds are planted in early spring and are best harvested before hot weather arrives. They can be grown during the fall as well but need more protection from frost than the rutabaga does. Turnips are not a fussy vegetable and will grow in most soil conditions. Both rutabagas and turnips store well in a root cellar or in similar conditions.

LEEKS

Leeks require growing conditions similar to other alliums, such as garlic and onions, which are discussed in the herb chapter. These conditions are rich soil, a sunny area, and cool temperatures. Leeks are a biennial vegetable, which means they do not produce seeds until the second year of growth. If you are planning to save your leek seeds, this is something you will need to take into consideration.

Leeks can take four to eight months to grow to prime size, which is usually about 1½ inches in diameter. They will produce tender young plants in the first year, but growing them into the second year will give you a longer harvest. Plant them on the edge of your garden or mixed in with your asparagus patch where they won't be disturbed. Keep mounding the soil up around the plant as it grows to keep the bottom part of the leek a nice white color.

When harvesting your leeks, gently lift them from the ground using a garden fork. The best way to store leeks is to leave them in the ground over the winter. You won't be able to access them once the ground freezes, but the following spring you will have a super early vegetable to harvest and enjoy. Make sure they are mounded with soil and mulched with a good covering of chopped leaves or straw to protect them in cold weather. To prepare leeks for cooking, wash them thoroughly to get the soil out from between the leaves.

HEAT-LOVING VEGGIES

These heat-loving veggies are mainly known as semitropical vegetables, and they need a lot of heat and warm soil to grow well. Soil temperatures must be warm for the seeds to germinate, and the plants cannot handle any cold weather, especially during the seedling stage. In northern climates, these vegetables usually need to be started indoors in early spring and then transplanted outside once the weather is warm enough.

CORN

Freshly picked corn dropped into a pot of boiling water is sweeter than anything you can buy in the supermarket because the sugar within the kernels has not yet turned to starch. Corn is a vegetable that can be planted in a newly cultivated garden area. It is hardy and tough, giving it the ability to grow and survive where many other vegetables would not. Corn does take up a fair amount of garden space, but it is definitely worth finding a place for in your backyard garden.

There are many different varieties of corn. For any of them to be successful, they need lots of space, warm weather, fertile soil, and water. Each cornstalk will produce one or two cobs, so you need a large garden area to plant your corn in order to get a good quantity of cobs. Corn likes a rich, warm soil (above 50°F) and needs at least eight hours of sunlight a day to germinate. It is best planted on the northern side of your garden so it does not block the sun from reaching your other vegetables.

Corn needs to be pollinated, meaning the male flowers from the tassels need to reach the female flowers (the silk on the ears). Usually the wind accomplishes this. It is best to plant corn in blocks; that way, the corn pollen from the tassels of one plant can easily spread to other plants. When choosing your varieties, make sure they cannot cross-pollinate, which can affect the health and taste of your harvest. It is best to choose only one variety of corn if you have a small garden. If you have a larger garden and choose to grow different varieties, make sure there is some distance between each variety, or choose to plant varieties that will mature at different times.

Corn tastes best when eaten fresh, but it is still worthwhile to preserve. You can easily freeze the kernels for several months. You can also dry corn on the cob and use the individual cobs for popcorn. These dried cobs will last for several months to a year but can't be used for anything other than popcorn.

CUCUMBERS

Cucumbers need to be pollinated, so it is important to know whether the variety you choose is a hybrid or a standard. Standard varieties have both male and female flowers on the same vine; insects or the wind will do the pollinating for you. The male flower comes out first and looks like a miniature cucumber. The female flower is identified by a swollen ovary just behind the male flower. Hybrid varieties have separate female and male plants and will need to be pollinated by hand. If you have saved cucumber seeds from the past or a friend has given them to you and you are not sure of the variety, check the plant as it grows to see what kind of flowers it is producing.

If there is only a male or a female flower, no fruit will form. Go to your garden center and purchase another plant that will pollinate the first one for you.

Cucumbers can be preserved in a brine and then either frozen or canned. You can use these pickled and frozen cucumbers in salads year-round, as their pickled flavor is milder than the more traditional, canned pickles.

EGGPLANTS

Eggplants need hot weather and rich soil in order to grow their best. This vegetable is much more common in Europe than it is in North America; however, if you enjoy a great moussaka or eggplant parmesan, try growing eggplants in your backyard or in a container on the patio. Eggplants are in the same family as tomatoes and peppers, so if you plant them in the same area it is easier to do your vegetable rotation.

The most common eggplant variety produces a large, purple, oval-shaped fruit. You can also find varieties that have yellow, green, or white fruit and others that form rounded or cylindrical fruit. These can all add color to your garden and are definitely fun to show off to your guests.

If you live in a cool climate, it is best to start your eggplants from seed indoors in early spring and then transplant them outside when warmer weather arrives. Eggplants need full sun and lots of heat, so they are an ideal candidate for a greenhouse or a more sheltered but sunny spot in your garden. Each plant will produce eight to ten fruits.

PEPPERS

Peppers come in various shapes, from chunky to long and skinny, and round to conical. You'll find them in shades of green, red, orange, and yellow. Their flavors range from mild and sweet to sizzling hot. Sweet peppers are also known as bell peppers because of the shape of the fruit. They are often harvested when green; that way, the plant produces more fruit. When left on the plant to mature, bell peppers will turn either yellow, orange, or red depending on the variety. Hot pepper plants grow taller and have narrower leaves than the bell varieties, and their fruit can range in size from about 1 to 7 inches long.

Peppers are a little touchy to grow. They need lots of full sun, warm daytime temperatures, cool nighttime temperatures, fertile soil, and lots of water. Sweet peppers need a little less heat than hot pepper varieties. When preparing your garden bed, add compost or aged animal manure. Peppers can then be seeded directly if you have a long growing season; however, they often do better if started indoors in early spring and transplanted outside once the temperature reaches 65°F.

Peppers are a very popular vegetable, either cooked by themselves or with other foods. They are also eaten raw in salads or as appetizers. When preparing to use your pepper, cut it in half, remove the stem, and rinse away the seeds. Fresh or dried hot peppers need to be handled carefully because the oils in the pepper skin can burn your skin or eyes. Consider wearing rubber gloves and holding the hot pepper under water when preparing it. Remove the seeds from a hot pepper if you want to cut down the heat; the seeds add to the hot taste.

Both sweet and hot peppers can be frozen, dried, or canned. If you're a fan of spicy foods, a dried string of your favorite hot peppers in your kitchen is both functional and pleasing to look at.

SQUASH

Squash is an easy vegetable to grow, and each plant can produce a large number of fruits. There are two types of squash: summer and winter. The main differences between these are the amount of time they take to mature and how well they will store once harvested. Summer squash is a warm-weather vegetable that is eaten before the fruit has fully matured. The skin and seeds are eaten as part of the whole fruit. Winter squash takes longer to mature and is usually harvested in the late summer or fall. It usually has a larger fruit than summer varieties and the skin is tough and inedible. The seeds are often removed before cooking as well. Some varieties, such as pumpkin squash, produce lovely edible seeds that are delicious when roasted.

Squash like a rich soil with plenty of organic matter. They often grow best in the compost pile. This vine vegetable can spread 6 to 8 feet across, so make sure you give them lots of room when planning your garden layout. Squash can be direct-seeded or put out as transplants, which usually depends on the length of your growing season. Each plant—especially the summer zucchini squash—can produce lots of fruit seemingly overnight, so one or two plants are usually enough for a family. Winter squash can also produce several fruits from one plant. If cured properly, they will store for several months so you can enjoy them over time.

Squash plants require lots of water. Because the leaves become very large, it is best to water the plant by hand or with drip irrigation around the base of the plant so the water reaches the roots. Squash leaves are susceptible to mildew if they get wet.

If cured properly, winter squash will store for several months. You cure squash by leaving the cut fruit in the sun for several days. You will need to turn the squash every few hours to ensure equal exposure. Protection at nighttime is also necessary and can be achieved either by covering or by bringing the fruit inside.

TOMATOES

There is nothing tastier than a ripe tomato that you have just picked off the vine. Tomatoes are one of the most popular vegetables eaten in North America, and most gardeners love to grow them. Most people think of a tomato as being round and red, but there are several varieties that produce yellow and orange fruit and others that produce fruit that is pear- or plum-shaped. The size of the tomato can range from 1 to 6 inches in diameter, depending on the variety you choose. One plant will produce an abundance of fruit for you to enjoy.

Tomatoes will grow well in any backyard so long as it is sunny and hot. They do well in containers and in greenhouses, especially if you live in a cooler climate.

Tomatoes are best started indoors, where you can regulate the temperature so they will germinate. Tomato seeds need ten to twelve weeks of growth before they are ready to be transplanted into the garden or a container. It is important that you harden off your tomato plants, introducing the plants to the cool outdoors gradually over several days' time when you are ready to transplant your tomato plants.

Unlike most plants, tomatoes like to be planted deep. Bury at least half of the stem underground to give the plant a strong root base. Tomatoes are best grown upright on supports. This allows the stem of the plant to grow tall without breaking from the weight of the fruit. It also keeps the fruit from touching the ground and allows air circulation around the plant.

Gardeners often give tomato plants either too much or too little water. When you first transplant a tomato plant, water it every few days until it is well established. Once the plant reaches 2 to 3 feet tall, the roots are probably just as deep; a little water each day will not reach where the roots need it the most. Tomatoes need a deep watering once a week or every ten days. Fruit that starts to split is one sign that the plant is not getting enough water.

If you are planning to grow your tomato plants in containers, it is best to choose dwarf or hanging varieties unless you have a very large container. A standard tomato needs a container at least 18 inches deep.

PRESERVE.

If you have lots of green tomatoes, try wrapping them in newspaper and keeping them in a cardboard box in a warm room. They will gradually ripen, giving you fresh tomatoes through the fall. Using this method, tomatoes harvested green in August may take until November to ripen—tasting just as fresh as if they had just been picked from the vine.

BRASSICAS

Also known as the cabbage family, this group of vegetables includes such favorites as broccoli, Brussels sprouts, cabbage, cauliflower, and kale. This section offers advice and growing tips for all these wonderful veggies. They are cold-hardy vegetables that produce a lot of food for the space they use. They grow well in most soil types. Adding shredded leaves to the area where you will be planting the following year will help to produce fabulous brassicas.

BROCCOLI

Broccoli is a cool-season crop and is probably the easiest of the brassicas to grow. Most varieties will produce one large head averaging about 6 to 8 inches in diameter. Once this head is cut off, the plant will continue to produce side branches with smaller heads. Keep cutting these before they flower and you will be able to harvest broccoli from one plant for several weeks.

The broccoli plant may bolt if the weather gets hot. This means the plant will go to flower more quickly than it normally would in cooler weather. It is best to plant broccoli early in the spring and then again in late summer if you have a mild fall and winter.

Broccoli often does best transplanted. This allows you to start your plants indoors so they get more growth before the heat of the summer arrives. The best way to store broccoli is by freezing. Before going into the freezer, broccoli should be soaked in saltwater to remove dirt and pests. After soaking for about thirty minutes, the broccoli can be chopped into smaller pieces.

BRUSSELS SPROUTS

When growing, Brussels sprouts look like little palm trees with lumps growing from the plant stem, or trunk. The bumps, which are usually 1 to 2 inches in diameter, are the Brussels sprouts. They are often called baby cabbages because they look like miniature cabbages. Each plant should produce between fifty and one hundred sprouts.

Brussels sprouts are a cool-season vegetable, and their taste is improved by a light frost. Like most brassicas, these vegetables like fertile, well-drained soil. This plant will produce into the fall, so long as it is harvested before the first frost. To store indoors, you want to leave the roots attached to the plants; hang them upside down in your root cellar as soon as they are harvested.

CABBAGE

Cabbage is another easy-to-grow vegetable in the brassica group. It grows well in most soils and is a cool-season crop. It is best to plant this vegetable in early spring for a summer harvest or in late summer for a fall harvest. The mature cabbage forms a head from a rosette of thickened leaves. The cabbage head can be round, pointy, or flattened depending on the variety. The leaves can be richly colored and textured. There are green varieties that produce light green leaves and red varieties with purplish-red leaves. The Savoy cabbage has crinkly leaves. There are short-season and long-season varieties.

Cabbage, like all brassica vegetables, is susceptible to a variety of soil-borne diseases, so crop rotation is essential in order to keep your garden healthy. Once you have planted brassicas in an area, do not plant them in that spot again until at least four years after the first crop. Like Brussels sprouts, cabbage can stay in your garden into the late fall and can be stored indoors in a root cellar or similar environment.

COOK.

Cabbage can be eaten cooked or raw. Sauerkraut (cooked cabbage) and coleslaw (raw cabbage) are two of the most common cabbage dishes. Cabbage contains a good amount of vitamin C and some vitamin A. Its nutritional and storage qualities make cabbage a common staple in many countries. Try cabbage in your soups, tacos, and burgers, either raw or cooked. A medium head of cabbage will give approximately 2 pounds of cabbage or about 12 cups of shredded cabbage.

COLLARDS

Collards are another cold-hardy vegetable in the brassica group. Their leaves look like cabbage leaves but do not form a head like a cabbage, and collards are grown to be cooked rather than eaten raw. Collards are usually planted in the summer for harvesting in the fall and winter. The leaves of a mature plant are sweeter after a frost. The collard plant can also take the heat, so it is one of the few cooking greens that will do well all summer long.

Collards need a rich soil and a lot of water in order for the leaves to stay tender. When working the soil, add 3 inches of compost or aged manure to the garden bed. Collards also do best with regular fertilization. Use a nitrogen-rich fertilizer every few weeks, which will give them the nutrients they need to grow fast, develop a nice green color, and taste tender.

KALE

Kale has high levels of vitamin C and calcium and the highest levels of beta carotene of all the green vegetables. A hardy vegetable, kale will survive over the winter, and the leaves are more tender and sweet once they have been touched by frost. Kale will easily go to seed and spread throughout your garden, so pull the plants out before the seeds spread if you want to contain it.

There are several different varieties of kale, which are easily distinguishable because of their colors and leaves. The most common are probably the green, curly-leaf varieties. Some other varieties are Red Russian, which have gray-green leaves with a purplish stem; Lacinato, or dinosaur, which has a dark blue-green leaf; Redbor, which has dark red leaves; and Improved Siberian, which has flat green leaves.

The Recipes

The following farm-to-fork recipes have been chosen because of how well they highlight vegetables that can easily be grown at home. Use them to get an idea of how to work with your garden's bounty and then adapt them to fit your personal tastes.

Parmesan Sprouts with Prosciutto

This is a deliciously rich way to enjoy these small brassicas! If you have the patience, wait to harvest your Brussels sprouts until after the first hard frost to ensure the best flavor.

Yields 4 servings as a side dish

2 tablespoons butter

2 cloves garlic, minced

2 ounces thinly sliced prosciutto, slivered

1 pound Brussels sprouts, cleaned and halved

1½ tablespoons all-purpose flour

1 cup cream

2 tablespoons port wine

Kosher salt and ground pepper to taste

⅓ cup freshly grated Parmesan cheese

1. Melt butter in a large frying pan over medium-high heat.
2. Add garlic and prosciutto. Simmer for 2 minutes, stirring regularly.
3. Add sprouts. Simmer for 5 more minutes.
4. Sprinkle flour evenly over the sprouts. Stir.
5. Slowly add cream, followed by the port wine. Simmer about 13 minutes until the sprouts are nearly fork tender.
6. Remove from heat; add salt, pepper, and half of the cheese, and stir well.
7. Store in freezer-safe containers. Label and date.

PRESERVE.

Once this dish is done, you can freeze it whole in an oven-ready dish or portion it out into individual servings. It will need to be cooked for 20 minutes at 350°F. Serve with additional freshly grated Parmesan cheese.

Vegetable Stock

Making vegetable stock is one of the handiest and most cost-efficient skills you can learn. You can adapt this recipe to use any extra vegetables, including the ends and parts of vegetables removed when preparing a meal.

Yields 8 quarts

14 quarts cold water
2 pounds peeled carrots, cut into 1-inch pieces
2 pounds peeled parsnips, cut into 1-inch pieces
1 bunch leeks, rinsed well and chopped fine
12 stalks celery, cut into 1-inch pieces
3 large onions, peeled and quartered
4 large sweet red peppers, seeded and cut into 1-inch pieces
4 large tomatoes, seeded and diced
4 medium turnips, peeled and diced
6 cloves garlic, peeled and minced
6 bay leaves
2 teaspoons dried thyme
1 cup fresh parsley, chopped
1 tablespoon black peppercorns
2 teaspoons fine sea salt

1. Combine all ingredients in a large stockpot. Bring to a boil.
2. Cover and reduce heat to low. Simmer for 2 hours.
3. Uncover and simmer for 2 additional hours to concentrate flavors.
4. Strain stock through several layers of cheesecloth in a colander. Discard veggies and seasonings.
5. If canning, ladle stock into sterilized jars, leaving 1 inch of headspace. Wipe rims. Cap and seal. Process in a pressure cooker at 10 pounds pressure for 30 minutes for pints or 35 minutes for quarts.

Tomato, Mushroom, and Barley Soup

This rustic recipe is a classic. You can substitute any other grains for the barley, just be sure to cook them first.

Yields 4 servings

1 tablespoon olive oil
1 cup chopped onion
⅔ cup chopped carrot
1 cup sliced celery
1 teaspoon dried savory leaves
1 quart water
16 ounces coarsely chopped tomatoes
Juice from the tomatoes
1 cup quick-cooking barley
2 cups sliced white or cremini mushrooms
Salt and pepper to taste

1. Over medium heat, heat olive oil in a saucepan until hot. Add onion, carrots, and celery, and cook just until onion is tender. Stir in herbs and cook for 1 more minute.
2. Add the water, tomatoes with their juices, barley, and mushrooms. Heat until boiling. Cover and cook for 10–15 minutes or until barley is tender. Remove from heat and add salt and pepper to taste.

Roasted Red Pepper Pesto

The combination of roasted red peppers and pesto creates a perfect summertime flavor. This recipe can be made in larger batches to freeze. Toss with pasta to add color and flavor to your favorite meals.

Yields 4 servings

1 cup roasted red peppers (see sidebar)
1 cup packed fresh basil
3 cloves garlic
¼ cup grated Parmesan
1 teaspoon balsamic vinegar
3 tablespoons olive oil
Optional: 1 teaspoon sugar
Salt and pepper to taste

1. Process all ingredients in food processor (don't add salt and pepper yet) until smooth.
2. Season with salt and pepper.
3. Mix with pasta or use as a spread.

COOK.

To roast any sweet pepper, simply cut in half and remove the seeds. Place skin side up on baking sheet and broil until the skins turn black. You can rub olive oil on the peppers prior to broiling, which will help the skins to come off, but you should wrap the peppers in aluminum foil to prevent burning.

Cream of Broccoli Soup

A comforting meal, enjoy this soup in the wintertime, using frozen broccoli and dried herbs.

Yields 6 servings

1 tablespoon olive or canola oil

1 cup chopped onions

3 garlic cloves, minced

2 pounds broccoli, cleaned and cut into 1-inch pieces

½ teaspoon dried thyme leaves

1½ cups vegetable stock

½ cup light cream

Salt and pepper to taste

Optional: 6 tablespoons sour cream

Optional: 3 tablespoons milk

1. Heat oil in a large saucepan until hot.
2. Add onions and garlic and cook for a few minutes until tender.
3. Add broccoli and thyme and cook for 2 minutes.
4. Add stock and heat until boiling. Then reduce heat, cover, and simmer for 10 minutes or until broccoli is tender.
5. Process the soup in a blender or food processor until smooth.
6. Return to saucepan, add cream, and heat over medium heat until hot enough to serve. Add salt and pepper to taste. If desired, you can combine the sour cream and milk and add to individual bowls of soup just before serving.

Summer Squash Pasta

This fast and easy summertime dish is a great way to use up some of the zucchini and summer squash from your garden!

Yields 4–6 servings

6 tablespoons olive oil
1 hot red pepper, sliced in half without seeds
2 garlic cloves
4 cups sliced summer squash or zucchini
1 cup fresh flat-leaf parsley, minced
Sea salt to taste
½ pound pasta

1. Heat oil in a skillet until hot.
2. Add pepper and garlic, and cook until the garlic turns a golden color. Take the skillet off the heat and remove the garlic and pepper, keeping the now-flavored oil in the pan.
3. Reheat the oil, add the squash slices, and fry for several minutes.
4. Take off the heat and add parsley and sea salt.
5. Meanwhile, boil water for the pasta. Once boiling, cook the pasta until it is al dente.
6. Drain and rinse pasta under cold water, then mix with the squash-parsley sauce.

Sesame Carrot Salad

This recipe is a great way to use your freshly harvested carrots during the summer, or carrots pulled from your root cellar during the colder months. This dish can be served warm, but it is also very good chilled and goes well as a side dish with soups or rice dishes.

Yields 4–6 servings

2 teaspoons sesame oil

2 teaspoons tamari soy sauce

1 teaspoon sea salt

1 cup orange juice

1 tablespoon rice syrup

3 tablespoons roasted, unhulled, black sesame seeds

3 cups shredded or very thinly sliced carrots

1. Combine all ingredients except sesame seeds and carrots in a saucepan and bring to a boil. Cover and simmer for 5 minutes.
2. Meanwhile, gently roast the sesame seeds just long enough to release flavor.
3. When the sauce and seeds are done, combine all the ingredients and serve either warm or chilled.

Eggplant Baba Ganoush

You can use this delicious Eggplant Baba Ganoush as a spread on crackers or bread, or like any other sandwich spread.

Yields 1 cup

2 medium eggplants
3 tablespoons olive oil, divided
2 tablespoons lemon juice
1 cup tahini
3 cloves garlic
1 teaspoon cumin
Optional: 1 teaspoon chili powder
1 teaspoon salt
1 tablespoon chopped fresh parsley

1. Preheat oven to 400°F. Slice eggplants in half and prick several times with a fork.
2. Place on a baking sheet and drizzle with 1 tablespoon olive oil. Bake for 30 minutes or until soft. Allow to cool slightly.
3. Remove inner flesh and place in a bowl.
4. Using a large fork or potato masher, mash eggplant together with remaining ingredients until almost smooth.
5. Adjust seasonings to taste.

Basil Bruschetta Pesto

You can use this bruschetta pesto as a dip for crusty bread, or you can top halved fresh bread with it, drizzle olive oil on top, and toast in the oven. Either way, it's a delicious, fresh, farm-to-table appetizer.

Yields 4 appetizer servings

2 large tomatoes, diced small
3 cloves garlic, minced
¼ cup chopped fresh basil
2 tablespoons olive oil
Salt and pepper to taste

Combine all ingredients in a bowl and allow to sit for at least 15 minutes so it can marinate. You may also add a little balsamic vinegar if preferred.

Fried Zucchini Sticks

You don't have to deep-fry these zucchini sticks, just sauté them in a bit of oil if you prefer. This is a great snack for kids!

Yields 4 servings

¾ cup flour
1 garlic clove, minced
1 teaspoon fresh basil, minced
½ teaspoon fresh oregano, minced
¼ teaspoon salt
4 zucchinis, cut into strips
Oil for frying
Ranch dressing or ketchup for dipping

1. In a large bowl or pan, combine flour, garlic, basil, oregano, and salt.
2. Lightly toss the zucchini strips with the flour mixture, coating well.
3. Heat oil in a large skillet or frying pan. When oil is hot, gently add zucchini strips to pan.
4. Fry until lightly golden brown on all sides. Serve with ranch dressing or ketchup.

Broccoli and Pasta Herb Soup

This is a great wintertime recipe that can be made with frozen broccoli and dried herbs. It can also be made in the summertime with fresh broccoli and fresh thyme.

Yields 4 servings

5½ cups vegetable stock
4 garlic cloves, minced
2½ teaspoons dried thyme leaves
3 cups broccoli florets
2½ cups fusilli pasta, uncooked
½ cup lemon juice
Salt and pepper to taste

1. Heat the veggie stock, garlic, and thyme in a saucepan and bring to a boil.
2. Stir in broccoli and pasta, and reduce heat.
3. Simmer uncovered for 10 minutes or until pasta is al dente and the broccoli tender.
4. Add the lemon juice, salt and pepper, and serve.

Zucchini Salad with Lemon Pepper Dressing

This recipe's simplicity and fresh taste make it a perfect summer dish. It is also a great zucchini recipe to add to your repertoire during prolific zucchini harvests.

Yields 4 servings

LEMON PEPPER DRESSING

1 mashed garlic clove

2 tablespoons fresh lemon juice

1 tablespoon wine vinegar

½ cup olive oil

Dash of sugar

Dash of sea salt

½ teaspoon cracked pepper

ZUCCHINI SALAD

4 small zucchinis

¾ cup Lemon Pepper Dressing

2 teaspoons dried oregano, or 2 tablespoons fresh oregano

8 large lettuce leaves, Boston lettuce works well

1. **For Lemon Pepper Dressing:** Stir all ingredients together vigorously.
2. **For Zucchini Salad:** Wash zucchini and remove the ends. Slice thinly lengthwise, mix with dressing and oregano, and allow to marinate for several hours at room temperature. Serve on lettuce leaves.

Pico de Gallo

Combining fresh, homegrown tomatoes, cilantro, onions, and garlic, this salsa is tastier by far than anything you can buy at the store.

Yields 1½ cups

2 good-sized tomatoes
1 medium yellow onion
1 bunch cilantro
1 or 2 limes
Salt and pepper to taste
Optional: ½–1 tablespoon honey
Optional: 1 teaspoon tamari soy sauce

1. Chop tomatoes and onion uniformly into small, but not fine, pieces.
2. Finely chop a bunch of cilantro, adding more or less depending on your taste. Combine with tomatoes and onion in a bowl.
3. Roll the lime(s) on the table or countertop to help release juices. Quarter lime(s) and squeeze as much juice as possible into the mixture.
4. Add salt and pepper to taste.
5. Add more lime juice if necessary. Depending on the variety and quality of your ingredients, adding honey and soy sauce can help to bring out the flavor. Try adding a little to taste.

Spicy German Dijon Potato Salad

This tangy deli-style German potato salad requires potatoes that are thinly sliced and not overcooked. This vegan version is just as good—if not better—than any other recipe you'll find.

Yields 4 servings

4 large potatoes, precooked and cooled
½ yellow onion, sliced thin
2 tablespoons olive oil
⅓ cup water
⅓ cup white or apple cider vinegar
1 tablespoon Dijon mustard
1 tablespoon flour
1 teaspoon sugar
2 scallions, chopped
Salt and pepper, to taste

1. Slice potatoes into thin coins and set aside.
2. In a large skillet, heat onions in olive oil over medium heat and cook until just barely soft, about 2–3 minutes.
3. Reduce heat and add water, vinegar, mustard, flour, and sugar, stirring to combine. Bring to a simmer and cook until thickened, just 1–2 minutes.
4. Reduce heat and stir in potatoes and scallions. Season with salt and pepper to taste.

Cucumber Cilantro Salad

Cool cucumbers and cold, creamy yogurt are coupled with a dash of cayenne pepper for a salad that keeps you guessing.

Yields 3 servings

4 cucumbers, diced
2 tomatoes, chopped
½ red onion, diced small
1 cup soy yogurt, plain or lemon flavored
1 tablespoon lemon juice
2 tablespoons chopped fresh cilantro
Salt and pepper to taste
Optional: ¼ teaspoon cayenne

1. Toss together all ingredients, stirring well to combine.
2. Chill for at least 2 hours before serving to allow flavors to marinate. Toss again just before serving.

Lemon Cumin Potato Salad

A mayonnaise-free potato salad with exotic flavors, this recipe is delicious either hot or cold.

Yields 4 servings

1 small yellow onion, diced
2 tablespoons olive oil
1 teaspoon cumin
4 large cooked potatoes, chopped
3 tablespoons lemon juice
2 teaspoons Dijon mustard
1 scallion, chopped
1 teaspoon cayenne pepper
Optional: 2 tablespoons chopped fresh cilantro

1. Heat onions in olive oil just until soft. Add cumin and potatoes, and cook for just 1 minute, stirring well to combine. Remove from heat.
2. Whisk together the lemon juice and Dijon mustard, and pour over potatoes, tossing gently to coat. Add scallions, cayenne pepper, and cilantro, and combine well.
3. Chill before serving.

Spicy Sweet Cucumber Salad

Japanese cucumber salad is cool and refreshing, but with a bit of spice. Enjoy it as a healthy afternoon snack or as a fresh accompaniment to takeout.

Yields 2 servings

2 cucumbers, thinly sliced
1 teaspoon salt
1 cup rice wine vinegar
1 teaspoon sugar
1 teaspoon sesame oil
1 teaspoon red pepper flakes
1 onion, thinly sliced

1. In a large, shallow container or baking sheet, spread cucumbers in a single layer and sprinkle with salt. Allow to sit at least 10 minutes.
2. Drain any excess water from the cucumbers.
3. Whisk together the rice wine vinegar, sugar, oil, and red pepper flakes.
4. Pour dressing over the cucumbers, add onions, and toss gently.
5. Let sit at least 10 minutes before serving to allow flavors to mingle.

Pesto and New Potato Salad

A simple side dish if served hot, or a tasty potato salad if served cold, these creamy pesto potatoes are a lively and creative way to use tender new potatoes.

Yields 4 servings

1 cup pesto
1 cup mayonnaise
2 pounds new potatoes, chopped and cooked
3 scallions, chopped
⅓ cup sliced black olives
Salt and pepper, to taste

1. Whisk together pesto and mayonnaise, and toss with potatoes and remaining ingredients.
2. Season generously with salt and pepper to taste.

Barley Vegetable Soup

This barley and vegetable soup is an excellent "kitchen sink" recipe, meaning that you can toss in just about any fresh or frozen vegetables or spices you happen to have on hand.

Yields 6 servings

1 onion, chopped
2 carrots, sliced
2 ribs celery, chopped
2 tablespoons olive oil
8 cups vegetable broth
1 cup barley, uncooked
1½ cups frozen mixed vegetables
1 14-ounce can crushed or diced tomatoes
½ teaspoon parsley
½ teaspoon thyme
2 bay leaves
Salt and pepper to taste

1. In a large soup pan or stockpot, sauté the onion, carrot, and celery in olive oil for 3–5 minutes, until onions are almost soft.
2. Reduce heat to medium-low, and add remaining ingredients except salt and pepper.
3. Bring to a simmer, cover, and allow to cook for at least 45 minutes, stirring occasionally.
4. Remove cover and allow to cook for 10 more minutes.
5. Remove bay leaves, and season with salt and pepper to taste.

Potato and Leek Soup

With simple, earthy flavors, this classic soup is a comforting starter. Enjoy it whenever you need a bit of comfort food.

Yields 6 servings

1 yellow onion, diced
2 cloves garlic, minced
2 tablespoons olive oil
6 cups vegetable broth
3 leeks, sliced
2 large potatoes, chopped
2 bay leaves
1 cup whole milk
2 tablespoons butter
¾ teaspoon salt
⅓ teaspoon black pepper
½ teaspoon sage
½ teaspoon thyme

1. Sauté onions and garlic in olive oil for a few minutes until onions are soft.
2. Add vegetable broth, leeks, potatoes, and bay leaves, and bring to a slow simmer.
3. Allow to cook, partially covered, for 30 minutes until potatoes are soft.
4. Remove bay leaves. Working in batches as needed, purée soup in a blender until almost smooth, or to desired consistency.
5. Return soup to pot and stir in remaining ingredients. Adjust seasonings and reheat as needed.

Easy Roasted Tomato Soup

Use the freshest, ripest, juiciest red tomatoes you can find for this super-easy recipe, as there are few other added flavors. If you find that you need a bit more spice, add a spoonful of nutritional yeast, a dash of cayenne pepper, or an extra shake of salt and pepper.

Yields 4 servings

6 large tomatoes
1 small onion
4 cloves garlic
2 tablespoons olive oil
1¼ cups soy milk
2 tablespoons chopped fresh basil
1½ teaspoons balsamic vinegar
¾ teaspoon salt
¼ teaspoon black pepper

1. Preheat oven to 425°F.
2. Slice tomatoes in half and chop onion into quarters. Place tomatoes, onion, and garlic on a baking sheet and drizzle with olive oil.
3. Roast in the oven for 45 minutes to 1 hour.
4. Carefully transfer tomatoes, onion, and garlic to a blender, including any juices on the baking sheet. Add remaining ingredients and purée until almost smooth.
5. Reheat over low heat for just 1–2 minutes if needed, and adjust seasonings to taste.

Curried Pumpkin Soup

This Curried Pumpkin Soup tastes delicious when you use the onion, garlic, and pumpkin straight from the garden. It's also excellent with coconut milk instead of soy milk.

Yields 4 servings

1 yellow onion, diced
3 cloves garlic, minced
2 tablespoons butter
2 cups pumpkin purée
3 cups vegetable broth
2 bay leaves
1 tablespoon curry powder
1 teaspoon cumin
½ teaspoon ground ginger
1 cup soy milk
¼ teaspoon salt

1. In a large soup pan or stockpot, heat onion and garlic in butter until onion is soft, about 4–5 minutes.
2. Add pumpkin and vegetable broth and stir well to combine. Add bay leaves, curry, cumin, and ginger, and bring to a slow simmer.
3. Cover and allow to cook for 15 minutes.
4. Reduce heat to low and add soy milk, stirring to combine. Heat for just another minute or two until heated through.
5. Season with salt to taste and remove bay leaves before serving.

COOK.

There's nothing like fresh-roasted pumpkin from your own garden! Make your own purée to substitute for canned. Carefully chop your pumpkin in half, remove the seeds (save and toast those later), and roast for 45 minutes to an hour in a 375°F oven. Cool, then peel off the skin, and mash or purée until smooth. Whatever you don't use will keep in the freezer for next time.

Cream Cheese and Butternut Squash Soup

This is a rich, decadent soup—a wonderful comforting treat in the middle of winter. Top with a mountain of homemade croutons or serve with crusty French bread.

Yields 4 servings

2 cloves garlic, minced
½ yellow onion, diced
2 tablespoons olive oil
3½ cups vegetable broth
1 medium butternut squash, peeled, seeded, and chopped into cubes
1 teaspoon curry powder
¼ teaspoon nutmeg
¼ teaspoon salt
4 ounces cream cheese

1. In a large skillet or stockpot, sauté garlic and onions in olive oil until soft, about 3–4 minutes.
2. Reduce heat to medium-low and add vegetable broth, squash, curry powder, nutmeg, and salt. Simmer for 25 minutes until squash is soft.
3. Working in batches, purée until almost smooth, or to desired consistency. Or, if squash is soft enough, mash smooth with a large fork.
4. Return soup to very low heat and stir in cream cheese until melted, combined, and heated through. Adjust seasonings to taste.

Fiery Basil, Eggplant, and Tofu Stir-Fry

Holy basil, also called tulsi, is revered in Vishnu temples across India and is frequently used in Ayurvedic healing. It lends a fantastically spicy flavor, but whatever basil you have in your garden will do.

Yields 3 servings

3 cloves garlic, minced

3 small fresh chili peppers, minced

1 block firm or extra-firm tofu, pressed and diced

2 tablespoons olive oil

1 eggplant, chopped

1 red bell pepper, chopped

⅓ cup sliced mushrooms

3 tablespoons water

2 tablespoons soy sauce

1 teaspoon lemon juice

⅓ cup fresh Thai basil or holy basil

1. Sauté the garlic, chili peppers, and tofu in olive oil for 4–6 minutes until tofu is lightly golden.
2. Add eggplant, bell pepper, mushrooms, water, and soy sauce, and heat, stirring frequently, for 5–6 minutes, or until eggplant is almost soft.
3. Add lemon juice and basil, and cook for another 1–2 minutes, until basil is just wilted.

Sesame Soy Asparagus and Mushrooms

Fresh asparagus in season has such a vibrant taste that, if you have an asparagus crop, you should give this recipe a try. Fresh asparagus needs very little enhancement. If you can't find fresh asparagus, don't bother trying this with dull store-bought asparagus; it's not the same at all!

Yields 4 servings

1 pound fresh asparagus, trimmed and chopped
¾ cup chopped mushrooms
2 teaspoons sesame oil
1 teaspoon soy sauce
½ teaspoon sugar
Optional: 2 tablespoons sesame seeds

1. Preheat oven to 350°F.
2. Place asparagus and mushrooms on a baking pan and roast for 10 minutes.
3. Remove pan from oven; drizzle with sesame oil, soy sauce, and sugar, and toss gently to coat.
4. Roast in oven for 5–6 more minutes.
5. Remove from oven, and toss with sesame seeds, if desired.

Cajun Collard Greens

Like Brussels sprouts and kimchi (Korean sauerkraut), collard greens are one of those foods that folks tend to either love or hate. They're highly nutritious, and this recipe will turn you into a fan if you're not one already.

Yields 4 servings

1 pound collard greens, chopped
1 onion, diced
3 cloves garlic, minced
2 tablespoons olive oil
¾ cup water or vegetable broth
1 14-ounce can diced tomatoes, drained
1½ teaspoons Cajun seasoning
½ teaspoon hot sauce (or to taste)
¼ teaspoon salt

1. Give your collards a good rinse, then tear the leaves off the middle stem.
2. Fold or roll all the leaves together, then run a knife through them to create thin strips, similar to a chiffonade cut used for herbs. The stems can be added to a vegetable broth or to your compost pile.
3. In a large skillet, sauté onions, garlic, and collard greens in olive oil for 3–5 minutes, until onions are soft.
4. Add water or vegetable broth, tomatoes, and Cajun seasoning. Bring to a simmer, cover, and cook for 20 minutes, or until greens are soft, stirring occasionally.
5. Remove lid, stir in hot sauce and salt, and cook, uncovered, for another 1–2 minutes, to allow excess moisture to evaporate.

Lemon Mint New Potatoes

Potatoes are an easy standby side dish that goes with just about any entrée. This recipe with fresh mint adds a twist to the usual herb-roasted version.

Yields 4 servings

10–12 small new potatoes, chopped
4 cloves garlic, minced
1 tablespoon olive oil
¼ cup chopped mint
Salt and pepper to taste
2 teaspoons lemon juice

1. Preheat oven to 350°F. Line or lightly grease a baking sheet.
2. In a large bowl, toss together the potatoes with the garlic, olive oil, and mint, coating potatoes well.
3. Arrange potatoes on a single layer on a baking sheet. Roast for 45 minutes.
4. Season with salt and pepper, and drizzle with lemon juice just before serving.

Summer Squash Sauté

Green zucchini and yellow squash absorb flavors like magic, though little enhancement is needed with their fresh, natural flavor. Toss these veggies with some cooked orzo or linguini to make a main dish.

Yields 2 servings

1 onion, chopped
2 cloves garlic, minced
2 tablespoons olive oil
2 zucchinis, sliced into coins
2 yellow squash, sliced thin
1 large tomato, diced
1 teaspoon dried oregano
1 teaspoon dried basil
Salt and pepper to taste
Optional: 2 teaspoons hot chili sauce

1. Sauté onions and garlic in olive oil for a minute or two, then add zucchini, yellow squash, and tomato. Heat, stirring frequently, for 4–5 minutes until squash is soft.
2. Season with oregano, basil, salt, and pepper and heat for 1 more minute.
3. Stir in hot sauce as desired.

Garlic Green Beans

Perfectly balancing the crispness of green beans with the bite of garlic, this recipe will liven up any serving of green beans.

Yields 4 servings

1 pound fresh green beans, trimmed and chopped
2 tablespoons olive oil
4 cloves garlic, minced
½ teaspoon crushed red pepper flakes
Salt and pepper to taste

1. Boil green beans in water for just 3–4 minutes, or steam for 4–5 minutes; do not overcook. Drain and rinse under cold water.
2. Heat olive oil in a skillet with garlic, green beans, and red pepper flakes. Cook, stirring frequently, for 3–4 minutes until garlic is soft.
3. Taste, and season lightly with salt and pepper.

Sweetened Roast Squash

Naturally sweet squash is delicious in this simple, quick, sustainable side dish. Serve as is, scooping squash out of the skin, or remove the soft flesh and give it a quick mash.

Yields 4 servings

1 butternut, acorn, or spaghetti squash
1 teaspoon sea salt
4 tablespoons orange juice
4 tablespoons maple syrup
Nutmeg or ginger to taste

1. Preheat oven to 400°F.
2. Chop squash in quarters, and scrape out seeds. Place in a large casserole dish. Sprinkle each chunk of squash with a bit of sea salt, 1 tablespoon orange juice, and 1 tablespoon maple syrup, then a shake of nutmeg or ginger.
3. Cover with foil and bake for 40–45 minutes until squash is soft, basting once or twice with any extra sauce.

Steamed Rosemary-Pepper Squash

Sweet butternut squash is delicious with just a touch of seasoning. This lightly seasoned squash recipe is easy to make, simple, and delicious.

Yields 4 servings

1 butternut squash
3 tablespoons olive oil
1 teaspoon sea salt
2 teaspoons dried rosemary, finely chopped
2 teaspoons freshly ground black pepper

1. Chop squash in half lengthwise, and scrape out seeds. Place in a large casserole dish. Drizzle olive oil on the flesh side. In a small bowl, combine the salt, rosemary, and black pepper; mix. Sprinkle each half of the squash with the seasoning.
2. Place the seasoned squash halves cut-side up in a stovetop pan large enough to hold them lengthwise and deep enough to add water without it boiling over. Pour in a couple inches of water, cover, and heat over medium-low heat.
3. Steam for 40–45 minutes until squash is soft.

Baked Potato Fries

Brown sugar adds a sweet touch to these homegrown potato fries. If you like your fries with a kick, add some crushed red pepper flakes or a dash of cayenne pepper to the mix.

Yields 3 servings

4 or 5 large potatoes, sliced into fries
2 tablespoons olive oil
¼ teaspoon garlic powder
½ teaspoon paprika
½ teaspoon brown sugar
½ teaspoon chili powder
¼ teaspoon sea salt, plus more as needed

1. Preheat oven to 400°F.
2. Spread potatoes on a large baking sheet and drizzle with olive oil, tossing gently to coat.
3. In a small bowl, combine remaining ingredients. Sprinkle over potatoes, coating evenly and tossing as needed.
4. Bake in oven for 10 minutes, turning once. Taste, and sprinkle with a bit more sea salt if needed.

Maple-Glazed Roasted Veggies

These easy roasted veggies make an excellent holiday side dish. The vegetables can be roasted in advance and reheated with the glaze to save time. One large potato can be substituted for the parsnips, if desired.

Yields 4 servings

3 carrots, chopped
2 small parsnips, chopped
2 sweet potatoes, chopped
2 tablespoons olive oil
Salt and pepper to taste
⅓ cup maple syrup
2 tablespoons Dijon mustard
1 tablespoon balsamic vinegar
½ teaspoon hot sauce
Optional: Extra salt and pepper

1. Preheat oven to 400°F.
2. On a large baking sheet, spread out chopped carrots, parsnips, and sweet potatoes.
3. Drizzle with olive oil and season generously with salt and pepper. Roast for 40 minutes, tossing once.
4. In a small bowl, whisk together maple syrup, Dijon mustard, balsamic vinegar, and hot sauce.
5. Transfer the roasted vegetables to a large bowl and toss well with the maple-syrup mixture. Add more salt and pepper to taste.

Roasted Garlic, Zucchini, and Onions

Roasting veggies brings out their natural flavors, so little additional seasoning is needed.

Yields 4 servings

6 whole garlic cloves
4 zucchinis, chopped
1 onion, cut into rings
1 tablespoon balsamic vinegar
1 tablespoon olive oil
Salt and pepper, to taste
1 teaspoon fresh thyme
Optional: 2 teaspoons nutritional yeast

1. Preheat oven to 400°F.
2. Arrange the garlic, zucchinis, and onion on a baking sheet. Drizzle with vinegar and oil, and season with salt and pepper, tossing to coat well.
3. Roast in oven for 20–25 minutes, then toss with fresh thyme, nutritional yeast, and additional salt and pepper to taste.

Dried Tomato Risotto
with Spinach and Pine Nuts

The tomatoes carry the flavor in this easy risotto—no butter, cheese, or wine is needed. But if you keep truffle, hazelnut, pine nut, or another gourmet oil on hand, now's the time to use it, instead of the butter.

Yields 4 servings

2 tablespoons olive oil
Optional: 2 tablespoons butter
1 yellow onion, diced
4 cloves garlic, minced
1½ cups Arborio rice, uncooked
⅔ cup rehydrated dried tomatoes, minced
½ cup fresh spinach
5–6 cups vegetable broth
¼ cup pine nuts
Salt and pepper to taste
Optional: 1 tablespoon chopped fresh basil

1. Heat the oil and butter in a large saucepan or deep fry pan over medium heat. Add onion, cooking for 1–2 minutes before adding the garlic. Cook the garlic for another 1–2 minutes but do not let it turn brown.
2. Stir in the uncooked rice and allow to cook for 3–4 minutes, being careful to not let it burn.
3. Stir in the tomatoes and spinach and allow to cook for 3 minutes, stirring frequently.
4. Pour in the vegetable broth, 1 cup at a time. Allow the rice to absorb each cup of broth by stirring and cooking for 3 minutes between each cup.
5. Once all the liquid has been absorbed you can turn off the heat and stir in the pine nuts.
6. Add salt and pepper and top with basil.

Spanish Artichoke and Zucchini Paella

Traditional Spanish paella is always cooked with saffron, but this version with zucchini, artichokes, and bell peppers uses turmeric instead to produce the same golden hue.

Yields 4 servings

3 cloves garlic, minced
1 yellow onion, diced
2 tablespoons olive oil
1 cup white rice, uncooked
1 15-ounce can diced or crushed tomatoes
1 green bell pepper, chopped
1 red or yellow bell pepper, chopped
½ cup artichoke hearts, chopped
2 zucchinis, sliced
2 cups vegetable broth
1 tablespoon paprika
½ teaspoon turmeric
¾ teaspoon parsley
½ teaspoon salt

1. In the largest skillet you can find, heat garlic and onions in olive oil for 3–4 minutes, until onions are almost soft. Add rice, stirring well to coat, and heat for another minute, stirring to prevent burning.
2. Add tomatoes, bell peppers, artichokes, and zucchinis, stirring to combine. Add vegetable broth and remaining ingredients, cover, and simmer for 15–20 minutes, or until rice is done.

Latin Rice with Corn and Peppers

This rice recipe loads up the veggies, making it hearty enough for a main dish. You can easily use your frozen or canned veggies if fresh ones aren't available.

Yields 4 servings

2 cloves garlic, minced
1 cup rice, uncooked
2 tablespoons olive oil
3 cups vegetable broth
1 cup tomato paste (or 4 large tomatoes, puréed)
1 green bell pepper, chopped
1 red bell pepper, chopped
Kernels from 1 ear of corn
1 carrot, diced
1 teaspoon chili powder
½ teaspoon cumin
⅓ teaspoon oregano
⅓ teaspoon cayenne pepper (or to taste)
⅓ teaspoon salt

1. Add garlic, rice, and olive oil to a large skillet and heat on medium-high heat, stirring frequently. Toast the rice until just golden brown, about 2–3 minutes.
2. Reduce heat, and add vegetable broth and remaining ingredients.
3. Bring to a simmer, cover, and cook until liquid is absorbed and rice is cooked, about 20–25 minutes, stirring occasionally.
4. Adjust seasonings to taste.

Mushroom and Rosemary Wild Rice

This earthy and fragrant dish is a wonderful comfort food and can be served as either a side dish or as a main course. It can also be used as a stuffing for a turkey or chicken; just add bread!

Yields 4 servings

1 tablespoon chopped fresh rosemary
1 yellow onion, diced
2 tablespoons olive oil
1 cup sliced mushrooms
1½ cups wild rice, uncooked
4½ cups vegetable broth
2 tablespoons butter
½ teaspoon lemon juice
¼ teaspoon ground sage

1. In a large pan, heat rosemary and onion in olive oil until onions are just soft, about 3 minutes. Add mushrooms, and heat for another minute.
2. Add wild rice and vegetable broth, and bring to a simmer. Cover and cook 40–45 minutes until rice is done and liquid is absorbed.
3. Remove from heat and stir in remaining ingredients.

Spinach Pesto

A flavorful twist on traditional pesto, spinach pesto is a great way to make a thicker and more flavorful sauce or spread. Use this pesto as a pasta sauce, or serve it on your favorite bread or crackers.

Yields 4 servings

1 cup loosely packed fresh spinach
3 tablespoons fresh basil, finely chopped
2 garlic cloves
1 tablespoon Parmesan cheese, grated
2 tablespoons olive oil
1–2 teaspoons lemon juice
Salt and pepper to taste

1. Mix all ingredients except lemon juice, salt, and pepper in a food processor until smooth.
2. Add lemon juice.
3. Allow the mixture to stand for 3 hours. Add salt and pepper to taste just before serving.

Squash and Sage Risotto

Risotto is easy to make, but it does take a bit of effort with all the stirring! This earthy recipe works well with just about any kind of squash that you can pick in your garden. You can also use any squash you have frozen or canned.

Yields 4 servings

3 cloves garlic, minced
½ yellow onion, diced
2 tablespoons olive oil
1½ cups Arborio rice, uncooked
5 cups vegetable broth
2 whole cloves
1½ cups roasted puréed pumpkin, acorn, or butternut squash
1½ teaspoons sage
⅓ teaspoon salt
¼ teaspoon pepper

1. In a large skillet, sauté the garlic and onions in olive oil for 3 minutes over medium-high heat. Add uncooked rice and cook for 2 more minutes, stirring frequently to lightly toast the rice.
2. Add ¾ cup vegetable broth and cloves, and stir well. When most of the liquid has been absorbed, add another ½ cup broth, stirring frequently. Continue adding vegetable broth ½ cup at a time until rice is just tender and sauce is creamy, about 20–25 minutes.
3. Reduce heat to medium-low and stir in puréed squash and ¼ cup vegetable broth. Continue to stir well and cook for 4–5 more minutes.
4. Stir in sage and season with salt and pepper.
5. Allow to cool, stirring occasionally, for at least 5 minutes. Risotto will thicken slightly as it cools. Remove cloves before serving.

Eggplant Puttanesca

Salty and garlicky puttanesca is a thick sauce traditionally served over pasta, but try it over a more wholesome grain, such as quinoa or brown rice.

Yields 4 servings

3 cloves garlic, minced
1 red bell pepper, chopped
1 eggplant, chopped
2 tablespoons olive oil
2 tablespoons capers, rinsed
⅓ cup sliced kalamata or black olives
½ teaspoon red pepper flakes
1 14-ounce can diced tomatoes
1 tablespoon balsamic vinegar
½ teaspoon parsley

1. In a large skillet or saucepan, sauté the garlic, bell pepper, and eggplant in olive oil for 4–5 minutes until eggplant is almost soft. Add capers, olives, and red pepper flakes, and stir to combine.
2. Reduce heat to low and add remaining ingredients. Cover and allow to simmer for 10–12 minutes until juice from tomatoes has reduced.
3. Serve over cooked pasta or rice.

Lemon Quinoa Veggie Salad

Depending on when you make this dish, you can use fresh or frozen veggies. Fresh broccoli and tomatoes work well.

Yields 4 servings

1½ cups quinoa
4 cups vegetable broth
1 cup frozen mixed veggies, thawed
¼ cup lemon juice
¼ cup olive oil
1 garlic clove, minced
½ teaspoon sea salt
¼ teaspoon black pepper
Optional: 2 tablespoons chopped fresh cilantro or parsley

1. In a large pot, simmer quinoa in vegetable broth for 15–20 minutes, stirring occasionally, until liquid is absorbed and quinoa is cooked. Add mixed veggies and stir to combine.
2. Remove from heat and combine with remaining ingredients. Serve hot or cold.

Baked Spinach Tart

Unlike the dull, dark leaves of spinach purchased in the frozen foods aisle at the grocery store, this mouthwatering tart featuring fresh greens from your garden is bursting with bright flavor and color.

Yields 4–6 servings

2 large eggs
1 cup plain nonfat or whole-milk yogurt
1 cup feta cheese
1 cup shredded mozzarella cheese
1 bunch fresh spinach, well rinsed, wilted, and chopped
½ cup chopped onion
Salt and freshly ground black pepper to taste
1 (9-inch) unbaked deep-dish pie shell
½ pint grape tomatoes

1. Preheat oven to 350°F.
2. Beat the eggs until foamy. Stir in the yogurt, feta cheese, mozzarella cheese, spinach, and onions, mixing well until combined. Season with salt and pepper.
3. Spoon the mixture into the pie shell and push the tomatoes into the top of the mixture.
4. Bake for about 40 minutes or until the mixture is firm to the touch. Let it cool slightly before slicing and serving.

Mediterranean Potato Salad

This potato salad works for all different varieties of potatoes. It's especially good if you've grown multiple varieties in your garden.

Yields 4 servings

2 pounds assorted potatoes, cooked and cooled
1 bunch scallions, thinly sliced
1 cup grape tomatoes
2 hard-boiled eggs, quartered
1 cup chopped Italian flat-leaf parsley
¾ cup pitted Niçoise olives
3 tablespoons bacon bits
2 tablespoons mayonnaise
2 tablespoons buttermilk
1 tablespoon olive oil
1 teaspoon smoked paprika
Salt and freshly ground black pepper to taste

1. Cut the potatoes up until they are of a uniform size. Put them into a salad bowl and add the scallions, grape tomatoes, eggs, parsley, olives, and bacon bits.
2. Whisk together the mayonnaise, buttermilk, olive oil, smoked paprika, salt, and pepper until well mixed. Dress the salad, tossing gently to coat all the ingredients.

Artichoke and Spinach Pesto Pasta

Spinach and artichokes with pesto is an impossibly delicious combination. This recipe tastes best when you use the ingredients straight from your garden.

Yields 4 servings

1 cup basil
1 cup spinach leaves
3 cloves garlic
½ cup pine nuts or walnuts
1 tablespoon lemon juice
⅓ cup nutritional yeast
½ teaspoon sea salt
¼ teaspoon pepper
2 tablespoons olive oil
1 cup chopped artichoke hearts
2 tablespoons butter
1 tablespoon flour
¾ cup milk
2 cups cooked pasta

1. Process together the basil, spinach leaves, garlic, nuts, lemon juice, nutritional yeast, sea salt, and pepper until almost smooth. Add olive oil, then artichoke hearts, and process until artichokes are finely diced.
2. In a small saucepan, melt the butter and stir in the flour to form a paste. Add milk, and heat until thickened.
3. Remove from heat and stir in basil and spinach pesto mixture.
4. Toss with prepared pasta and enjoy.

Lemon, Basil, and Artichoke Pasta

The earthy rosemary, basil, and lemon flavors would go well with gnocchi; otherwise use a grooved pasta, such as corkscrews, to catch the sauce.

Yields 6 servings

12 ounces pasta, cooked
1 6-ounce jar artichoke hearts, drained and chopped
2 large tomatoes, chopped
½ cup fresh basil, chopped fine
½ cup sliced black olives
2 tablespoons olive oil
1 tablespoon lemon juice
½ teaspoon rosemary
Salt and pepper to taste

Over low heat, combine the cooked pasta with the remaining ingredients, combining well and heating until just well mixed and heated through, about 3–4 minutes.

CHAPTER 4

FRUITS AND HERBS

E ven if you're looking to reap most or all of the ingredients that end up on your dining room table from your own garden, you still don't want to give up the fruits and herbs that bring sweetness and flavor to many dishes. Fortunately, you don't have to! In this chapter, you'll not only learn what types of fruits and herbs to plant, you'll also find a variety of farm-to-fork recipes that highlight these key ingredients and keep your taste buds happy.

FRUITS

Small fruits are a great way to introduce at-home fruit production to your garden and year-round food supply. Requiring little maintenance once established, small fruits are perennials and will satisfy your family's fruit needs for years to come. Extremely adaptable to container gardening and a wide range of hardiness zones, small fruit plants are easy to grow organically and can be incorporated into almost any home garden system. Planting fruit is also an investment, and for the gardener and food enthusiast, fruit grown at home will easily pay off in the decades during which many of these plants produce. Let's take a look at some of the fruits that you may want to plant in your garden.

STRAWBERRIES

Strawberries are a classic summer fruit and one of the easiest fruit plants to grow. Grown in small, bushy clusters, strawberries are perennials. Depending on climate variation and the particular type of strawberry, you can expect to get anywhere from two to five years, and sometimes longer, out of your plants. The strawberries that you grow yourself are by far superior to any strawberries that you can find at the grocery store and are a wonderful addition to your garden and year-round diet.

Planting Strawberries

Strawberries prefer full sun and nutrient-rich, slightly acidic soil. They are also serious nutrient consumers. The soil that your berries grow in needs to be replenished regularly in order to get the most productivity and longevity from your plants. Some growers go so far as to uproot their strawberry plants in the fall and keep them in containers during the winter, then add compost and organic matter to the soil before returning the berry plants to the ground in the spring. In colder zones this method is also useful as a way to ensure that your plants survive during winters with extreme temperatures, although in many zones, mulching is enough protection.

When planting these heavy-feeding berry plants, it is important to add organic matter to the soil a couple of weeks prior to putting the plants in the ground to ensure that your strawberries start off in a nutrient-rich soil. Adding organic fertilizers after the plants are in the ground is also helpful.

In addition to feeding your strawberry plants, it is also important to protect them from cold over the winter, extreme heat in summer, weed growth, and pests. Mulching is the best tool to cover most of these areas; a heavy application of a basic mulch (like straw or hay) will keep your roots cool during the heat of summer, offer protection from severe winters, and also limit weed growth.

Regular monitoring of your strawberry plants is important to keep away root-eating pests. The best way to control pests is by prevention. By removing rotting berries and unhealthy leaves, you can stay ahead of insect problems. Birds offer a more serious threat, but you can drape bird-proof netting over your strawberry plants when they begin to ripen.

Strawberry Runners

Strawberries are started from small plants that propagate by sending out runners. If allowed to extend themselves, these runners will help to continue your strawberry productivity and longevity by producing new young plants each year. For the healthiest and most productive strawberry crop, you should plant with enough space to allow these runners to grow. June-bearing varieties produce more runners than everbearing and day-neutral varieties and will therefore need more space. Best planted in rows, June-bearers should be spaced about 2 feet apart, with 3 to 4 feet between rows, whereas everbearing and day-neutrals only need to be spaced about ½ foot apart, with only 2 feet between rows.

GROW.

In order to maintain healthy and productive strawberry plants for years, it is necessary to thin your rows of berries by removing any older plants and leaves. You can do some of this by hand, but your work will be made easier if you also mow over your strawberries in order to thoroughly remove excess leaves. Be sure to set your mower at a high enough setting so as not to damage any plants. When you are done thinning, the remaining strawberry plants will need some extra attention. It's a good idea to add a considerable amount of fertilizer and put down new mulching.

Strawberry Varieties

There are three types of strawberries: the June-bearer, the everbearing, and the day-neutral. These berries all differ in flavor, in the quantity of their crops, and whether or not they produce only at one particular time during the year, rather than throughout the year. Both everbearing and day-neutrals can be harvested in their first year, whereas June-bearers cannot be harvested until their second year.

June-bearing strawberries produce one bumper crop of strawberries in late spring that is perfect for making a large batch of preserves. This variety is best known for its small berries, deep in color and intensely luscious in flavor. These little berries are a burst of flavor in your mouth and will remind you of warmer weather when you enjoy them in their preserved form in the wintertime. In addition to their concentrated flavor, June-bearers are the best strawberries for making preserves because all the berries on June-bearing plants will be ready at the same time. For the gardener who wants to keep a supply of berries through the winter, planting a crop of June-bearers will ensure a pantry full of fruit preserves. These berries can also be frozen. Don't expect them to retain their shape and appearance as well as the large, firm strawberries you can buy at the grocery store, but their delicious flavor will remain intact.

Everbearing berries produce three crops of berries throughout a season. They typically begin producing after June-bearers in early summer and will continue until the fall in most areas. This variety produces fewer berries than the other two but is still a popular fruit with gardeners because of its continual production throughout the season and because of its ability to adapt to most climates. The flavor of this berry is less intense, yet its consistency and continual growth will keep you in fresh strawberries throughout the summer.

Day-neutral strawberries are similar to the everbearing in that they produce throughout the summer. As the name suggests, this variety is not affected by day length, and will continue producing into the fall, ending the season with a plentiful crop. In general, day-neutrals produce more berries, with better flavor, than the everbearing variety. They do not, however, withstand high heat as well as the everbearing. For these reasons, both varieties are popular, and often one is better suited to your region than another.

Many gardeners plant all three of these varieties in order to have a continual supply of strawberries from spring until fall. Planting a combination of June-bearer, everbearing, and day-neutral types will ensure a good supply of strawberries beyond the warm weather if you plan to preserve the majority of your June-bearing crop.

Traditional strawberry preserves are a popular favorite and will keep well beyond the following June (if you can keep your family from eating them all!). Freezer jam is a popular, raw version of the traditionally canned, cooked jams. Cleaned and frozen whole strawberries are also useful to have on hand for smoothies, milkshakes, and pastry and cake toppings, as well as for any baking or cooking that calls for whole berries.

BLUEBERRIES

Blueberries are a favorite berry to grow, particularly in colder regions because of their ability to withstand severe winters. Blueberries are native to North America, and varieties that are adapted to many different regions are available. Because blueberries prefer full sun and are also extremely hardy, these plants are ideal for almost any climate. Including these lovely flowering bushes in your home garden is an easy way to enjoy homegrown fruit no matter where you live.

There are four different types of blueberries, most easily recognized by their differing heights: lowbush, highbush, half-high, and rabbiteye.

- **Lowbush:** Commonly referred to as wild blueberries, lowbush is the shortest type, reaching a height of up to 18 inches. These are the famous Maine blueberries, and are also popular in other cold climates. Lowbush blueberries are winter hardy as far north as hardiness zone 3. The recognizably small berries on these plants are intensely sweet and make wonderful preserves.
- **Highbush:** Highbush varieties produce the larger round berries that are commonly sold in grocery stores. These plants can reach 6 feet in height and prefer warmer temperatures. These berry plants are winter hardy in zones 4 and up.
- **Half-High:** Half-high varieties are hybrids and are a compromise between the temperature requirements and taste of the lowbush and highbush varieties. The berries are a medium size, and these plants are just as hardy as the lowbush variety, although the berries are not as intensely flavorful. True to their name, half-high blueberries are taller than lowbush, but not as tall as highbush varieties.
- **Rabbiteye:** Rabbiteye blueberries are the tallest type of blueberry plant. When well pruned, these bushes grow to around 10 feet tall; unpruned, up to 20 feet. Rabbiteye blueberries are best suited for zones 7 and higher because their thick skin protects berries from extreme heat. They are commonly grown in the Southwest and produce a berry not much larger than the lowbush varieties.

Soil Acidity

Success with blueberry plants has a lot to do with the care they receive in the first year they are planted, as well as with the soil they are planted in. One of the most important factors in growing blueberries is soil acidity. Blueberries will do best in soil with a pH between 4 and 5. Soil that has a pH higher than 5 will need to be amended before any plants can go in the ground. If you are working with soil with a pH significantly higher than 5 (7 and up, or alkaline), you should consider planting your blueberry plants in containers or raised beds.

In addition to the pH level, blueberries like a loose, moisture-retentive, sandy loam that also drains well. In order to maintain and fertilize the soil that your blueberries grow in, you can add any fertilizer that is specific to acid-loving plants.

Planting Blueberries

Most blueberries are self-pollinating, but productivity will be better if you enlist the help of bees by planting different varieties of berries.

For the home gardener looking to plant berries for more than just a tasty snack during the summer months, you will want to plant about two plants per person, or slightly less if you are planting many other types of berries. Because you will be planting more than just a couple of plants, it makes sense to plant your blueberries in rows so that you can dig a trench that will hold multiple plants, versus digging individual holes. You will also have more long-term success with soil health if you prep by the bed, and not by the hole.

Lowbush varieties need the least amount of space, and depending upon the variety, should be planted 1 to 3 feet apart with about 4 feet between rows. Because lowbush varieties have low-lying male parts, it's important to encourage runners to develop on the lowest level. When planting, cover the lowest part of the plants with a little bit of soil to encourage growth of these parts.

Highbush, half-high, and rabbiteye varieties should all be planted with about 5 feet between plants, and up to 10 feet between rows. These bushes should be planted 3 inches deeper than the root ball size.

Pruning Blueberries

Pruning is particularly important during your blueberry plant's first year. Pruning can seem daunting if you're new to it, but it's actually quite easy. It helps if you think of this task in terms of your general goal, which is to stimulate growth. By removing parts of the plant that require energy to sustain but that do not produce, you are enabling the plant to redirect energy into fruit production. Likewise, pruning excess or weakly producing parts helps the plant not to overproduce, which can weaken and shorten both the lifespan and long-term productivity of a blueberry plant.

Prune in the spring, and remove all nonvigorous and dead wood growth. Any stems that are more than an inch thick should be removed, as well as any low-achieving stems. Before winter, you'll also want to cut back any long canes that could potentially break under heavy snow.

In addition to removing woody excess, in the first year you want to remove any blossoms. You won't harvest blueberries in this first year, and you may not even see any flowers. If you do see blossoms, however, it's important to take them off because doing so allows the canopy to develop. In later years this will be important when yield, and therefore weight, on the plant increases. You'll need a strong canopy for support.

GROW

Blueberries require about 1 inch of water a week, and they like moist soil. Mulching is an effective tool in helping the plants to retain water, as well as limiting weed growth and providing root protection. A light mulch of pine needles, chips, or bark works well and also helps to maintain the acidity of the soil.

Pest Control for Blueberries

Blueberries are rarely and only minimally affected by insect damage or disease. Animals are more likely to cause damage, but it is fairly easy to prevent crop loss or plant damage as long as you plan ahead. Able to destroy an entire crop quickly, birds are by far the most destructive enemy to a blueberry crop. Most blueberry plants will have ripe berries for about three weeks. During these weeks, you can cover your blueberry bushes with bird-proof netting. Draping the netting on individual bushes works only moderately well, as birds can still get to the berries by going underneath the net. If you have enough bushes that it seems worth your while, then you might want to consider building a frame around your blueberry bushes. During the harvest season, you can enclose the frame with the same bird-proof netting. This will keep birds out as well as allow you inside for cultivation and harvesting.

The young, tender branches of blueberry plants are a wintertime food source for small animals and rodents as well as birds. Chicken fencing should suffice for protection, and if you decide to build a wooden frame for bird netting, chicken wire can easily be incorporated into this design to offer year-round protection. If you live in an area with heavy snowfall, build your fence high enough to account for the literal step up this snow will give small animals.

BRAMBLE FRUITS

Bramble fruits are the fruits produced on the thorny bramble plants that belong to the rose family. Raspberries and blackberries are the most popular bramble fruits for cultivation and consumption, and plants can continue producing for up to twenty years! Red raspberries are grown in every state except Hawaii; this plant's ability to grow in such a diverse array of climates is a testament to the many varieties available, as well as to the overall adaptability of this particular plant. Blackberries are more limited in their ability to grow in cold climates, but are still considered winter hardy to zone 6.

Bramble fruit plants are thorny bushes whose roots and crowns are perennial. The fruit-producing canes, however, operate on a biennial cycle, not producing fruit until their second year. Red raspberries are available in an everbearing variety that produces fruit twice on the same cane, first in the fall, then again the following summer. These varieties are also called primocane fruiters because of their ability to produce berries on the first-year cane.

Growing different types of bramble berries makes for a fun small-fruit garden that will offer a variety of tastes to your year-round diet. Depending on your hardiness zone, you may be able to grow all different types of bramble berries or just one or two varieties. Understanding what types grow best in your particular climate will help you to have a vibrant and productive fruit garden.

Red Raspberry

Easily the most hardy, red raspberries are commonly grown throughout North America. Part of their adaptability comes from the availability of everbearing and primocane varieties. In zones with severe winters, the summer crop on primocane varieties is often sacrificed by cutting back the canes after a fall harvest in order to prevent cold damage during the winter. The plant won't produce the following summer, but the canes will grow back in time to produce a bountiful fall crop.

Black, Purple, and Yellow Raspberries

Black raspberries are not as adaptable or high-producing as red raspberries. They tend not to be very winter hardy, although there are varieties available that are hardy in climates as cold as zone 3. Black raspberries are also more prone to disease than red raspberries. The flavor of these berries is recognizably different than red raspberry and typically less juicy.

Purple raspberries are next in line after red raspberries in winter hardiness. These berries are a hybrid of red and black raspberries. They are less susceptible to disease than black raspberries and can be almost as high-producing as red raspberries. Yellow raspberries are less common than the darker berries. They tend to have a taste similar to the red raspberry but sweeter.

Blackberries

Blackberries differ from raspberries in taste. The fruits are not hollow like raspberries are after harvesting. This is because blackberries do not separate from the receptacle like raspberries do. Some blackberry plants grow similarly to raspberry plants as thorny, self-erect bushes. Other blackberry varieties grow in trailing, semi-erect, thornless bushes. These thornless varieties are popular for home gardening and small-scale berry production as the added work of regular trellising is often outweighed by the appeal of thorn-free harvesting.

Planting Bramble Berries

Bramble berries prefer a slightly acidic and nutrient-rich soil. A pH between 5.5 and 6.2 is best for these plants, and adding organic matter to the soil before planting is a must. The soil should be fertilized annually as well. These plants prefer full sun and a well-draining, sandy loam for soil.

Although considered to be self-erect (aside from the trailing blackberries), you will need to provide structural support for your raspberry and blackberry plants. Red raspberries do well when planted as a hedgerow because they fill out evenly as they grow and act as supports for one another as the hedge fills in. For this reason, red raspberries can be planted 2 feet apart. As they mature, you will want to maintain a base width of 12–18 inches per plant. The plants should be trellised; a standard T trellis works well. The crossbar on the T should be about 3½–4½ feet tall and 3½ feet wide. Wire is attached to each end of the crossbar and positioned so as to enclose the row of plants while connecting the Ts at each end of the row.

Only red raspberries should be planted as a hedge, as other types of raspberries and blackberries do not fill out as well and should not be planted as close together.

Without the support of closely neighboring plants, these raspberries require a post to be positioned next to each plant. Plants and posts should be spaced at 4 feet, with wire connecting the posts at a height of 4½ feet. As the plants grow, you should assist them by placing fruiting canes on the connecting wire, and help to support canes by wiring them to the nearest post when necessary.

Disease and Pest Control for Bramble Fruits

Raspberries and blackberries are more susceptible to disease than other berries. It is important to select varieties that are disease resistant and certified virus-free. Your local small-fruit nursery is a good resource for learning which diseases to look for in your region, as well as which varieties of plants are most disease resistant. If you have wild raspberry or blackberry bushes growing in your area, these plants can carry disease to your bramble fruits. You should allow a distance of at least 600 feet between any wild plants and your domestic ones. It is better to plant your bramble berries a good distance away from the wild plants, rather than creating this distance by destroying the wild berries. Depending on your particular outdoor space, however, you may have to remove some wild plants.

Maintaining weed control will also help to keep pests and diseases away from your plants. To stay on top of weed control, you can use mulch or even cover crops. Be sure to pay attention to how these additions affect the pH levels. Good airflow is also important for disease prevention. By practicing regular pruning and by following the plant-spacing guidelines previously outlined, good airflow will be promoted.

HERBS

Herbs are an essential element in any meal and any garden. In food, they add flavor and provide healthful properties, and the right combination can turn a simple dish into a culinary work of art. At the heart of sauces and marinades, or on their own as a gentle dusting or heavy rub, herbs bring out the flavor and texture of whatever they are paired with. Many herb combinations are famous as flavors in themselves, and even more so than specific vegetables, herbs and the flavors they produce are linked to the cultures, regions, and people who have historically grown and cooked with them. If you're serious about eating well with what you grow yourself, then growing and preserving your own herbs is a must.

Aside from their postharvest use, herbs in the garden provide a balance of beauty and function. By adding to the diversity of what you grow, herbs add to the diversity and health of your soil. The birds and insects that are attracted to different varieties of herbs add to a healthy ecosystem, keeping one another in check. A garden that incorporates a variety of herbs looks more lush, diverse, textured, and colorful, and also smells wonderful. The aromatic and therapeutic qualities of herbs are reason enough to grow and preserve at least a few favorites.

In Chapter 1, you began thinking about the herbs that are staples in your home—the ones you use regularly and consistently throughout the year. Use these herbs as a base to get started planning your herb garden as they will take up the majority of your gardening space.

If herbs are already integral to your home, you may want to consider organizing your garden according to the different ways in which you use herbs, such as culinary herbs or herbs that you'll use for tea. Within each section, you'll want to grow some herbs to be used fresh, some to preserve, and some in larger quantities because they will be staples in your home. Designing your garden and thinking about your herbs according to these guidelines is helpful in understanding the quantities of herbs that you want to produce, which herbs you will preserve and how, as well as any herbs you will only use fresh.

CULINARY HERBS

Everyone's cooking style is different, and your culinary herb garden will be a reflection of your own unique cooking style. The following is a list of herbs that comprise a universally well-rounded and practical herb garden for culinary use. Adapt this list to meet your individual needs.

Basil

Common in many types of cuisine, basil is best eaten fresh; however, this herb is delicious enough in any form to be useful preserved as well. You can preserve basil by making and freezing pesto, as well as by drying and then crushing the leaves. Basil is an annual plant and can be easily grown indoors in the colder months. Keeping a few pots of fresh basil in your kitchen, as well as freezing and drying some, should be enough to keep even the most devout basil worshipper satisfied throughout the year.

Chives

Chives offer the popular and flavorful taste signature of the allium (garlic and onion) family. With a milder taste than onions, green onions, or scallions, chives are a wonderful addition to salads, dips, or any food improved by a gentle onion flavor. Chives are a perennial plant, and you can count on them to add beauty and taste to your herb garden year after year. Their hollow, green stalks are ready in early spring, and you can enjoy them in your meals well before most other alliums will be ready to harvest.

Cilantro and Coriander

Delicious in fresh salsas, marinades, soups, and anything else that you want to add a fragrant flavor to, cilantro is actually the leaves of the coriander plant. Coriander seed is produced and typically used as an ingredient in cakes, breads, and other sweet dishes. It also has a reputation as a digestion aid. Cilantro is important to Asian, Latin, and Caribbean cooking, and is best enjoyed fresh, although it can be dried or frozen in sauces and blended salsas.

Dill

Dill is an important herb to grow if you plan to incorporate pickling into your home food-preservation system. This herb grows easily, but has a root system that likes to grow deeply, so planting in well-aerated soil is best. In warm climates, dill is a biennial herb, although it is typically grown as an annual. Dill does not live for very long, so reseeding every few weeks is a good idea if you want a constant supply of this herb.

In addition to its use in brines and pickling recipes, fresh dill leaves are wonderful when paired with fish. Use them in soups, eggs, and veggie dishes, and in salads and sandwiches. Unfortunately, dill does not retain much flavor when dried. Freezing is the best way to preserve this herb, although it's best in its fresh form.

Garlic

Whereas most herbs are grown for their leaves or flowers, garlic is grown specifically for its flavorful bulb. One of the most powerful and recognizable flavors, garlic adds personality and pungency to any dish. Although it can be started from either seed or clove, garlic is more easily started from individual cloves. Garlic can be planted in either spring or late summer, but bulbs will grow larger and more successfully if planted a month or so before the first fall frost. This warmer period allows the roots to become established before the harshness of winter sets in. Garlic responds well to the cold, and bigger, more flavorful bulbs are produced when garlic grows over through the winter. Garlic does need to be mulched for protection from extreme cold. Depending on climate and soil variation, garlic can take 6 to 10 months to be ready to harvest, although the scapes can be harvested earlier (garlic scapes have a mild garlic flavor and are delicious to eat on their own, or cooked with other foods). You'll know the whole garlic plant is ready to harvest when the leaves lowest on the stalk turn brown and dry out.

Garlic can be eaten fresh as soon as it is harvested, but is most commonly seen in its cured, dried form because it stores so well. To cure garlic, do not clean the plant after harvesting, and leave the bulb attached to the stalk. Lay the plants out on a screen or other area that will allow for even air circulation and will keep the plants off the ground. It's best to do this when you can expect dry weather. After the plants have been cured for several days to a week, you can braid the stalks of the plants together and hang them in your pantry or kitchen. When braiding, leave enough room around each bulb to allow air circulation. You can simply cut a new bulb off this braid when you need more garlic.

Mint

There are many varieties of mint—all sharing the common traits of its signature fresh scent and a ferocious ability to quickly take over a garden! Spearmint is most commonly grown, although the type of mint you choose to grow depends on your personal taste. Mint is great in teas and fruit sauces and jellies, as well as for its pleasant scent. Take care to plant mint in containers, as it will quickly take over your garden or any space it is planted in. Mint is best preserved by drying.

Onion

Onion, like garlic, is grown for its bulb. The strong flavor of these bulbs is necessary to many different dishes and types of cuisine. There are many types of onions, and varieties of red, yellow, and white are most common. Onions can be seeded indoors in the early spring and are one of the first transplants that can go into the ground. They can also be seeded directly or started from bulbs. Unlike garlic, which grows best planted in individual stalks, onions can be planted in small bunches of three plants. This allows enough room for each bulb to grow, and makes for easier cultivation and harvesting.

Onions have a long shelf life and preserve extremely well. They should be cured in the same way as garlic—remaining dirty after being harvested and allowed to dry thoroughly before storing. The stalks of onion plants are not strong enough to braid well, however, and once the plant is dry, the stalks can be snipped off.

Oregano

A Greek herb and a member of the mint family, oregano is often used in combination with basil and other herbs common in Mediterranean cuisines. Oregano is a perennial, evergreen herb, but is not hardy enough to survive the winters of colder zones. This herb does not do well in full sunlight, preferring partial shade, and is best suited for well-draining soil. This herb can also be kept growing indoors during the colder months. The flavor of oregano intensifies in its dried form.

Parsley

Often underestimated, parsley is so much more than a garnish! Packed with nutrients, this herb is rich in antioxidants and has a vibrant flavor. Parsley comes in flat-leaf and curly-leaf varieties. Flat-leaf parsley has a stronger flavor and holds up better than curly varieties for preserving. Parsley can be dried or frozen, although its flavor is best when fresh. A biennial herb, parsley is more practically grown as an annual, as it becomes less desirable to cook with in its second year.

Rosemary

Rosemary is an evergreen herb, but it is not hardy enough in colder zones to survive an unprotected winter. Depending on your climate, you might need to cover your rosemary during the winter, bring it indoors, or simply uproot and dry the whole plant at the end of the season. Rosemary has a strong flavor, and even if you use it regularly, a typical cook can get away with producing and using a moderate amount of rosemary, unlike herbs that tend to be used in larger quantities, such as basil or cilantro.

Savory

Savory is an annual herb with many uses. Flavorful with a peppery kick, this herb comes in a lighter summer variety as well as a more intense winter variety. Summer savory is tender and can be used fresh in salads, whereas the coarser winter savory is most commonly cooked, particularly with vegetables, beans, and lentils. Wonderful to add to soups and stews, you can easily dry savory and use it year-round. Savory is also easily grown indoors.

Thyme

Thyme is a perennial, a member of the mint family, and comes in many varieties, although English and French are the most common for culinary use. Thyme's flavor goes well with meat and egg dishes and is equally useful in both its dry and fresh forms. Preferring well-draining soil and full sun, thyme is easy to grow and is a useful plant outside of its kitchen use. Fragrant and healthful, thyme is rich in antioxidants, has anti-inflammatory properties, and improves skin condition along with many other health and medicinal properties.

HERBS FOR TEA

Herbs are multifaceted plants, and in addition to adding delicious flavor and nutrition to meals, herbs also possess medicinal and therapeutic qualities. Often processed for their essential oils and fragrance, the therapeutic qualities of different herbs can be absorbed in different ways. Whether applied directly to the skin as a poultice or balm; inhaled through the steam of fragrant oil; dried, crushed, and put into capsules; or consumed as a tea, herbs are truly diverse in their uses and benefits.

The use of herbs as tea is described in this section. Many of the herbs described in the previous culinary section also have aromatic and therapeutic qualities and are enjoyable as teas. In particular, rosemary, thyme, and mint can be used in this capacity.

COOK.

To brew tea with loose herb cuttings, you will need a mesh tea ball. These come in different sizes and it's a good idea to have a single-serving tea ball as well as one large enough to brew a pot of tea. Most herbs should be brewed in hot water (not quite boiling) for 3–5 minutes. To make a more powerful infusion, allow herbs to steep for as long as 20 minutes. Whenever drinking herbal teas or herbal infusions, be cautious of the effects of these herbs, as well as the interactions between herbs, medications, and any health conditions that you have.

Catnip

Known for its popularity with cats, catnip is also useful to humans. Wonderful as a tea, catnip serves as both an antidepressant and as a sleep aid, as well as helping to fight off colds. This herb is a perennial and also a ferocious grower. Be sure to allow plenty of room for catnip to grow, otherwise it will overcrowd its neighboring plants. It's best to harvest the leaves of the plant just as the flowers begin to bloom. You can use the leaves fresh, dry, or frozen. With regular pruning, catnip plants will grow into full, bushy plants about 2 to 3 feet in size.

GROW.

The growing and harvesting of herbs is as old as civilization. The earliest known writings of most cultures reference herbs used in preparing food, preserving food, scenting the body, and treating wounds and illnesses. Some of the herbs used 2,000 years ago are still used in drugs that modern doctors prescribe today.

Chamomile

One of the most popular tea herbs, chamomile plants are low and bushy, and both the flowers and leaves are harvested and used for tea. The fresh flowers can also be used as an edible and healthful garnish on salads and other fresh dishes. Commonly used for its anti-inflammatory properties, specifically for skin ailments, chamomile can be ground and applied as a poultice, or added to bathwater to ease skin irritations. When drunk as a tea, chamomile is known for its relaxing effect on adults and also to ease teething and colic discomfort in babies.

Echinacea

Echinacea is famous for its ability to strengthen the immune system. It also grows a beautiful flower and is an attractive addition to any garden. Both the purple flower and the root of the plant can be used to make tea and balms. Echinacea plants like full or partial sun and well-drained soil. Cut just as the first flowers are beginning to bloom. Take care if cutting the root—you only want to remove a small portion, leaving enough for the plant to continue growing. Both the root and the flower can be dried easily.

Evening Primrose

Evening primrose is well known for its ability to aid women with menstrual discomfort as well as for relieving common skin irritations such as acne and eczema. The entire plant is edible—you can harvest the seeds, leaves, flowers, and even the roots.

To make tea, use the leaves and flowers in dried form. You can boil the roots or cook them as you would any other root crop. Evening primrose is a biennial, and if you want to get the most out of your plant, you should wait to harvest the roots until after the seeds have been produced. The leaves and shoots and even the flowers of evening primrose can be eaten fresh in salads. This plant produces a beautiful yellow flower that will bloom at dusk, in the evening, and on cloudy days, adding character to your garden.

Lavender

One of the most beloved fragrances, lavender is known for its ability to soothe, reduce stress and anxiety, and promote consistency in moods. Also recognized for its aid in treating headaches, lavender is most commonly used outside of the kitchen, although it does have some culinary use as an herbal tea. Lavender holds its fragrance extremely well in its dried form and should be harvested just as it begins to bloom in order to preserve the fragrance. Lavender enjoys full sun and dry soil, although it is an adaptable plant and different varieties will take better to different climates. Lavender is a perennial, but you can only expect to get about ten years out of a plant.

Lemon Balm

In warmer zones, lemon balm can be grown as a perennial if it is mulched. A member of the mint family, this herb is an aggressive grower, and like mint you might want to consider separating this plant from the rest of your garden. Lemon balm is traditionally used as a digestive aid and as a fever reducer. It is a favorite of bees and butterflies, and its essential oils contain citronella, which helps to keep away mosquitoes. Lemon balm should be harvested before it flowers. The leaves can be chopped up fresh and are a great addition to fruit and vegetable salads. To make tea, you can dry the herbs, or use them fresh. Lemon balm preserves well through drying or freezing, although the flavor is much stronger in its fresh form.

Lemon Verbena

Lemon verbena is known primarily for its scent. It is a deciduous perennial, meaning that its leaves fall off before winter, when it lies dormant. Lemon verbena is not a hardy plant and only in the warmest zones can you expect it to winter over. It can be planted in containers and brought indoors in the winter; the bare, woody stalks will not be the most attractive window plants, but you'll be happy you saved this herb come spring. The leaves of lemon verbena are harvested and are delicious in teas, and also pair well with rosemary and mint. Lemon verbena tea tastes wonderful, and is useful as an expectorant, a digestive aid, and a fever reducer. Lemon verbena can also be chopped up and added fresh to salads and salsas, or sprinkled on cooked dishes. Its fresh, lemony taste goes well in baked goods, particularly in sweet quick breads.

Herb Planting, Maintenance, and Harvest

All herbs are different, but they have many common needs. Most herbs will do well in soil lacking in fertility, as the lack of nutrients actually perpetuates the richness and depth of the essential oils in most herb plants. The root systems of many herbs can succumb to rot if planted in anything other than well-draining soil. Most herbs are best started indoors and raised to be transplanted into the garden, although you can successfully seed some herbs directly, depending on your climate.

Herbs, like any other plant, require consistent care in order to control weeds and pests. Additionally, herbs tend to require pruning, but because you will be harvesting regularly from your plants, most of the pruning needs will be taken care of. Prune and harvest evenly throughout the plant, allowing main branches to remain. Pinching off shoots and extra leaves will help the plant to become bushy and healthy, and reach its optimal mature size.

Most herbs are harvested for their leaves, and as a general rule of thumb it is best to harvest just before, or just as, the first flowers begin to bloom. This is when the essential oils (where most of the nutritional and healthful properties are contained) are at their most potent and flavorful. Harvest in the morning, after the dew has dried on the leaves and before the heat of the day dries the plants. If harvesting to preserve, the same holds true and you will have the best results if you harvest at the peak of oil production: just as the first flowers are starting to bloom.

The Recipes

The following recipes are delicious ways to enjoy your homegrown fruits and herbs. You may be surprised at how versatile these simple ingredients can be when you transform them into the following farm-to-table dishes.

Summer Strawberry Ice Cream

Homemade ice cream is a wonderful treat, especially during the warm months. If you want to personalize this recipe, try adding some flaked coconut to the egg yolk mixture or blend in raspberries.

Yields 4 cups

1¼ quarts fresh strawberries, hulled

1½ cups heavy cream, divided

¾ cup white sugar

½ teaspoon vanilla extract

3 egg yolks

3 tablespoons light corn syrup

1. Place the berries into a blender or food processor; purée until smooth.
2. Heat 1¼ cups cream in a saucepan over medium heat until it begins to bubble at the edge of the pan.
3. In a separate bowl, whisk together sugar, vanilla, egg yolks, remaining ¼ cup cream, and corn syrup.
4. Slowly pour the cream into the egg yolk mixture, whisking constantly.
5. Return the mixture to the saucepan. Simmer until mixture is thick enough to coat the back of a wooden spoon, about 5 minutes. Do not boil!
6. Mix berries and custard together; refrigerate until chilled.
7. Use an ice cream maker to get a really smooth dessert. If you don't have an ice cream maker, you can transfer the custard into a mixing bowl and put it in the freezer. After 30 minutes, beat thoroughly and return to freezer. Repeat until you achieve the desired texture.

Lavender Raspberry Jam

This recipe makes use of both the lavender and raspberries that you've grown. Properly stored, this jam will keep for a month.

Yields 2 pints

3 cups fresh or frozen, thawed raspberries
1 cup shredded dried lavender
2½ cups fine sugar

1. Mix the raspberries and lavender leaves in a glass or stainless-steel bowl. Refrigerate overnight.
2. In the morning, heat the raspberry-lavender mixture over low heat. Once the raspberries begin releasing their juices, bring the mixture to a boil.
3. Add the sugar and stir until dissolved. Boil for another 5 minutes over low heat, stirring constantly. Pour into jars.

Lavender Blueberry Jam

Making use of both your blueberries and lavender, this jam will store for a month.

Yields 2 pints

2 tablespoons dried lavender flowers
6-inch square of cheesecloth
10 inches of twine
1 11½-ounce can white grape juice concentrate
3 cups fresh blueberries

1. Put the dried lavender flowers into the middle of the cheesecloth square and tie into a bundle with twine.
2. Put the can of white grape juice concentrate, blueberries, and the bundle of lavender blossoms into a heavy saucepan. Boil gently for about 20 minutes, stirring constantly to prevent sugar from sticking.
3. Remove the lavender bundle and cool. You can check if the jam is done by putting a little bit on your finger to see if it jells. If it's not done, you can continue cooking over low heat until it is ready.
4. Once the jam is done, pour into jars. This jam will keep in the refrigerator for up to a month.

Vegan Whole-Wheat Blueberry Muffins

These rustic muffins are a healthier version of traditional blueberry muffins, and are more delicious when you incorporate your homegrown blueberries. Because these muffins have very little fat, they'll want to stick to the papers or the muffin tin. Letting them cool before removing them will help prevent this, and be sure to grease your muffin tin well.

Yields 1½ dozen muffins

2 cups whole-wheat flour
1 cup all-purpose flour
1¼ cups sugar
1 tablespoon baking powder
1 teaspoon salt
1½ cups soy milk
½ cup applesauce
½ teaspoon vanilla
2 cups blueberries

1. Preheat oven to 400°F.
2. In a large bowl, combine the flours, sugar, baking powder, and salt. Set aside.
3. In a separate small bowl, whisk together the soy milk, applesauce, and vanilla until well mixed.
4. Combine the wet ingredients with the dry ingredients, stirring just until mixed. Gently fold in half of the blueberries.
5. Spoon batter into lined or greased muffin tins, filling each about ⅔ full. Sprinkle remaining blueberries on top of muffins.
6. Bake for 20–25 minutes, or until lightly golden brown on top.

Raspberry Vinaigrette Dressing

Create a colorful and inviting salad with this purplish dressing. Dress up a plain fruit salad, or toss some cranberries, pine nuts, and baby spinach with this vinaigrette for a gourmet touch.

Yields 1¼ cups

¼ cup balsamic or raspberry vinegar
2 tablespoons lime juice
¼ cup raspberry preserves
2 tablespoons Dijon mustard
½ teaspoon sugar
¾ cup olive oil
Salt and pepper to taste

1. Process together vinegar, lime juice, raspberry preserves, mustard, and sugar in a food processor or blender until smooth.
2. Slowly add olive oil, just a few drops at a time on high speed, to allow oil to emulsify.
3. Season generously with salt and pepper.

Raspberry Salsa

This fruity salsa is great for snacking or as a topping for meat.

Yields 3 quarts

6 cups fresh raspberries
1¼ cups red onion, chopped
4 jalapeño peppers, seeded and finely chopped
1 large sweet red pepper, seeded and chopped
¾ cup cilantro, loosely packed and finely chopped
Juice and grated zest of 2 limes
½ cup white vinegar
4 tablespoons balsamic vinegar
3 tablespoons honey
3 cloves garlic, finely minced
1½ teaspoons ground cumin
½ teaspoon cayenne pepper
1 teaspoon ground coriander
½ teaspoon black pepper

1. Put half the raspberries in a large stockpot and mash lightly. Add the remaining raspberries and the remaining ingredients. Bring to a boil, stirring constantly to prevent scorching. Boil gently for 5 minutes.
2. Ladle into sterilized jars, leaving ¼ inch of headspace. Wipe rims. Cap and seal. Process in water-bath canner for 15 minutes.

Strawberries and Beets Salad

Colorful and nutritious, this vibrant red salad can be made with roasted or canned beets, or even raw grated beets if you prefer.

Yields 4 servings

3 or 4 small beets, chopped
Water for boiling
Spinach or other greens
1 cup sliced strawberries
½ cup chopped pecans
¼ cup olive oil
2 tablespoons red wine vinegar
2 tablespoons honey
2 tablespoons orange juice
Salt and pepper to taste

1. Boil beets in water until soft, about 20 minutes. Allow to cool completely.
2. In a large bowl, combine spinach, strawberries, pecans, and cooled beets.
3. In a separate small bowl, whisk together the olive oil, vinegar, honey, and orange juice, and pour over salad, tossing well to coat.
4. Season generously with salt and pepper, to taste.

Blueberry Cobbler

A delicious and traditional way to use your blueberries year-round. This mouthwatering dish will have your kitchen smelling like summertime no matter the season.

Yields 8–10 servings

COBBLER TOPPING

1½ cups flour (either all-purpose or whole-wheat pastry)

⅓ cup sugar

1 teaspoon baking powder

½ teaspoon baking soda

½ teaspoon salt

6 tablespoons butter

½ cup buttermilk

½ teaspoon vanilla

BLUEBERRY COBBLER

6 cups fresh blueberries

⅓ cup light brown sugar, plus more for sprinkling

¼ cup flour

Grated zest of 1 lemon

1 tablespoon fresh lemon juice

1 tablespoon molasses

Cobbler Topping

1 egg, beaten

1. **For Cobbler Topping:** Combine flour, sugar, baking powder, baking soda, and salt.
2. Using a large fork or a pastry cutter, cut in 6 tablespoons butter.
3. Stir in ½ cup buttermilk and ½ teaspoon vanilla.
4. **For Blueberry Cobbler:** Preheat oven to 375°F and lightly butter an 8-inch × 10-inch baking dish.
5. Toss the berries with the brown sugar, flour, lemon zest, lemon juice, and molasses. Put the mixture in the baking dish and cover with the Cobbler Topping.
6. Brush with the egg and sprinkle brown sugar on top. Bake for about 25 minutes, or until the fruit starts to bubble at the edges.
7. Serve warm with vanilla ice cream.

Berry Jam Bars

These bars are a favorite snack that can be packed for school lunches or hiking trips, or served as an after-dinner treat.

Yields approximately 20 bars

½ cup butter
½ cup powdered sugar
½ cup light brown sugar
1 teaspoon vanilla
1 egg
½ teaspoon baking powder
½ teaspoon ground cinnamon
1½ cups flour
¼ teaspoon salt
½–¾ cup raspberry preserves
¾ cup rolled oats

1. Preheat oven to 350°F.
2. Cream butter with sugars until light and fluffy. Beat in the vanilla and egg, and mix until smooth.
3. Add the remaining ingredients except for the preserves and oats. Save ¾ of the dough and spread the rest into an 8-inch × 10-inch baking dish. Spread the preserves on top.
4. Mix the leftover dough with the oats and sprinkle on top. Bake about 40 minutes or until lightly browned.
5. Cool and cut into bars.

Lavender Jam

This homegrown Lavender Jam is so delicious, you'll be happy to pass the recipe around to your friends.

Yields 2 pints

Handful of dried lavender blossoms
¼ cup sugar
⅔ cup port wine
⅔ cup crème de cassis
½ cup water

1. Mix together all ingredients and then bring to a slow, gentle boil in a saucepan until the liquid becomes syrupy, stirring occasionally to prevent sticking. This should take about 30 minutes.
2. Pour into a glass jar and refrigerate.

Garlic Bread Spread

A classic way to make use of your garlic, you can keep this spread on hand for fast and delicious garlic bread any time. The refrigerated lifespan of this blend is eight weeks. To use this spread, lightly butter a whole loaf of bread and then add this spread on top. Heat under the broiler until cheese melts, about 1 minute.

Yields 5–6 pints

6 cups shredded mozzarella cheese at room temperature
1½ cups grated Parmesan cheese
1½ cups grated Romano cheese
1 tablespoon coarsely ground black pepper
1 cup minced garlic
1 cup extra-virgin olive oil
2 teaspoons freshly squeezed lemon juice

1. In a large mixing bowl, add 3 cups mozzarella cheese and half of each of the remaining ingredients. Using a large spatula, fold until blended.
2. Repeat with remaining ingredients.
3. Put into sterilized pint Mason jars. Put on sterilized lids and bands. Keep refrigerated.

Herb Garlic Blend

Mix this Herb Garlic Blend with butter for garlic bread beyond compare. This farm-to-fork blend is sure to impress your guests and leave them wanting more.

Yields 1 cup

4 tablespoons minced basil
4 tablespoons tarragon
4 tablespoons chervil
5 tablespoons minced thyme
1 teaspoon garlic powder

1. Put all ingredients into a blender or food processor; whirl until fine.
2. Store in a jar with an airtight cover.

Garlic Onion Pesto

This is the foundation for a great white pizza. Just brush it over the crust and add your favorite toppings from your garden.

Yields about 3 cups

2 cups fresh basil, packed
¼ cup pine nuts
¼ cup dried minced onion
⅛ cup minced garlic
¼ cup olive oil
1 tablespoon lemon juice

1. Place all ingredients into a nonreactive pan over a low flame; simmer 15 minutes.
2. Cool; transfer to ice cube trays. Freeze.
3. Pop out frozen pesto cubes and put in a food-storage bag in the freezer.

Garlic Stock

Have fun experimenting with different types of garlic in this broth. For a milder but rich garlic taste, bake the garlic in olive oil before using it for the stock.

Yields 6 cups

1½ tablespoons olive oil
½ head garlic, peeled and chopped
½ head elephant garlic, peeled and chopped
6 cups vegetable stock
1 bay leaf
¼ teaspoon dried thyme
Pinch of dried sage
Salt to taste
Pepper to taste

1. Warm the oil in a frying pan and very lightly sauté garlics.
2. Combine all ingredients; boil.
3. Reduce heat; simmer 30 minutes.
4. Strain; taste for saltiness.
5. Preserve as desired. If canning, use 10 pounds of pressure for 30 minutes for pints.

Garlic Quinoa

This farm-to-fork dish is a simple way to spruce up plain quinoa when served as a side dish, or as a topping to cooked veggies.

Yields 4 servings

1 yellow onion, diced
4 cloves garlic, minced
2 tablespoons olive oil
1½ cups quinoa
3 cups vegetable broth
½ teaspoon salt

1. In a large skillet, heat onion and garlic in oil or margarine for 3–4 minutes until onions are soft.
2. Add quinoa and vegetable broth, and bring to a simmer. Cook for 15 minutes until liquid is absorbed.
3. Fluff quinoa with a fork and stir in salt.

Quinoa and Fresh Herb Stuffing

Substitute dried herbs if you have to, but fresh are best to use in this untraditional stuffing recipe.

Yields 6 servings

1 yellow onion, chopped
2 ribs celery, diced
¼ cup butter
1 teaspoon chopped fresh rosemary
2 teaspoons chopped fresh marjoram
1½ tablespoons chopped fresh thyme
1 tablespoon chopped fresh sage
6 slices dried bread, cubed
1¼ cups vegetable broth
2 cups cooked quinoa
¾ teaspoon salt
½ teaspoon pepper

1. Preheat oven to 400°F.
2. Heat onion and celery in butter and cook until soft, about 6–8 minutes. Add fresh herbs and heat for another minute, just until fragrant.
3. Remove from heat and add bread, combining well. Add vegetable broth to moisten bread; you may need a bit more or less than 1¼ cups.
4. Add cooked quinoa, salt, and pepper, and combine well.

Bulgur Wheat Tabbouleh Salad
with Tomatoes

Though you'll need to adjust the cooking time, of course, you can try this tabbouleh (also called tabouli) recipe with just about any whole grain. Bulgur wheat is traditional, but quinoa, millet, or amaranth will also work.

Yields 4 servings

1¼ cups boiling water or vegetable broth
1 cup bulgur wheat
3 tablespoons olive oil
¼ cup lemon juice
1 garlic clove, minced
½ teaspoon sea salt
½ teaspoon pepper
3 scallions, chopped
½ cup chopped fresh mint
½ cup chopped fresh parsley
3 large tomatoes, diced

1. Pour boiling water over bulgur wheat. Cover and allow to sit for 30 minutes, or until bulgur wheat is soft.
2. Toss bulgur wheat with olive oil, lemon juice, garlic, and salt, stirring well to coat. Combine with remaining ingredients, adding in tomatoes last.
3. Allow to chill for at least 1 hour before serving.

Lemon Cilantro Couscous

This flavorful couscous is a light and easy side dish, or top it with a vegetable stew or some stir-fried or roasted veggies.

Yields 4 servings

2 cups vegetable broth
1 cup couscous
⅓ cup lemon juice
½ cup chopped fresh cilantro
¼ teaspoon sea salt, or to taste

1. Bring vegetable broth to a simmer and add couscous. Cover and let stand for 10 minutes, until soft; then fluff with a fork.
2. Stir in lemon juice and cilantro, and season generously with sea salt.

Fresh Basil Pomodoro

Pick out the finest fresh zucchinis and tomatoes in your garden for this recipe, as pomodoro is a simple pasta dish with little added flavor.

Yields 4 servings

2 zucchinis, sliced
4 cloves garlic, minced
2 tablespoons olive oil
4 large tomatoes, diced
⅓ cup chopped fresh basil
2 cups prepared angel hair or spaghetti pasta
Salt and pepper to taste
Parmesan cheese

1. Heat zucchini and garlic in olive oil over low heat for just a minute or two until zucchini is just lightly softened. Add tomatoes and cook for another 4–5 minutes.
2. Toss zucchini and tomatoes with basil and pasta, and season with salt and pepper, to taste. Serve topped with a sprinkle of Parmesan cheese.

Savory Sage Pasta

The earthy rosemary and sage flavors in this dish will complement gnocchi well. Make your own out of your homegrown potatoes!

Yields 6 servings

12 ounces pasta, cooked
½ cup fresh sage, chopped fine
½ cup sliced cooked bacon
2 tablespoons cream
1 tablespoon butter
½ teaspoon rosemary
Salt and pepper, to taste

Over low heat, combine the cooked pasta with the remaining ingredients, combining well and heating just until well mixed and heated through, about 3–4 minutes.

Lemon Thyme Orzo with Asparagus

If you have fresh thyme growing indoors when your asparagus is ready to harvest, this recipe is a perfect way to welcome this early spring veggie. The combination of lemon and thyme is understated and rustic, and will also work well with dried thyme. If you aren't growing asparagus, use this recipe later in the season with green peas or lightly steamed broccoli.

Yields 4 servings

1½ cups orzo
1 bunch asparagus, chopped
2 tablespoons olive oil
Zest from 1 lemon
2 tablespoons lemon juice
½ teaspoon salt
¼ teaspoon pepper
2 teaspoons chopped fresh thyme

1. Cook orzo according to package instructions.
2. In a large skillet, heat asparagus in olive oil until just tender. Do not overcook.
3. Reduce heat to low and add orzo and remaining ingredients, stirring to combine well. Cook for just a minute or two, until heated through, and adjust seasonings to taste.

Lemon Verbena Sherbet

A light and refreshing dessert, Lemon Verbena Sherbet is the perfect end to any summer meal. The homemade version gives a blast of rich flavor that you simply cannot buy in a store.

Yields 1 quart

2 cups whole milk
2 cups lemon verbena leaves, plus more for garnish
½ cup sugar, plus 2 tablespoons more
Pinch of salt
½ cup lemon juice
Extra lemon verbena leaves for garnish

1. In a saucepan, bring the milk, lemon verbena leaves, sugar, and salt to a slow boil.
2. Remove from heat and allow to stand for one hour. Stir occasionally.
3. After an hour, strain the liquid and add the lemon juice.
4. Freeze in an ice cream maker and garnish with lemon verbena leaves.

Parsley Salad

Parsley is delicious and flavorful in this extremely simple dish, and it tastes even better when you have the satisfaction of picking it off the plant right before cooking.

Yields 2 servings

2 cups fresh parsley, packed
2 tablespoons extra-virgin olive oil
1 teaspoon fresh-squeezed lemon juice (or more to taste)
Sea salt and pepper to taste

1. Toss parsley lightly with olive oil.
2. Season with lemon juice, salt, and pepper. Enjoy!

Freshly Herbed Beets

This recipe can be served with strong-flavored cheese or dill cheese as a tasty complement.

Yields 6–8 servings

1½ pounds cooked and peeled beets
2 tablespoons red onion, finely chopped
2 tablespoons chopped fresh parsley
2 tablespoons chopped fresh cilantro
1 tablespoon chopped fresh mint
Finely ground zest of 1 lemon, and 2 tablespoons juice
6 tablespoons extra-virgin olive oil
Salt and pepper
4 handfuls salad greens, such as spinach, frisée, red leaf lettuce, or a combination

1. Quarter the beets.
2. Whisk together onion, herbs, lemon zest and juice, oil, salt, and pepper in a small bowl.
3. Taste the dressing on a beet and adjust to your preference. Toss the beets with just enough dressing to lightly coat them.
4. Use the remaining dressing to toss with salad greens.
5. To serve, arrange the salad on plates and add the beets.

Parsley and Mint Carrot Salad

This Parsley and Mint Carrot Salad is a fast and easy way to showcase your fresh carrots and herbs.

Yields 6–8 servings

1 pound peeled and grated carrots
1 tablespoon fresh lemon juice or white wine vinegar
2 tablespoons olive oil
Small handful of chopped fresh parsley
Couple pinches of finely chopped mint leaves
Salt and pepper

Toss all ingredients in large bowl. Add salt and pepper to taste.

Winter Herb Dressing

This classic dried-herb vinaigrette can be used at any time of year, but its conduciveness to dried herbs makes it ideal for wintertime when fresh herbs are harder to come by.

Yields approximately ¾ cup

1 clove garlic
¼ teaspoon peppercorn
¼ teaspoon fennel seeds
½ teaspoon dried tarragon
Pinch of salt
1–2 tablespoons dried parsley
Zest of 1 lemon
¼ cup thinly sliced scallions
⅓ cup extra-virgin olive oil
2 tablespoons champagne vinegar
Salt to taste

1. Using a mortar and pestle, make a smooth paste with the garlic, peppercorn, fennel, tarragon, a pinch of salt, and half of the parsley.
2. Combine with all the other ingredients except vinegar and salt.
3. Allow to sit for 30 minutes before adding the vinegar, and salt to taste.

Sweet and Spicy Sauce

This recipe is sure to become a favorite sauce to liven up plain rice, or as a dipping sauce or salad dressing.

Yields just under 1 pint

Rice vinegar
Olive or canola oil
1 dried chili pepper, ground
1 tablespoon honey
1 garlic clove, pressed or minced
½ teaspoon freshly grated gingerroot
Sea salt
Freshly ground black pepper

1. Using twice as much vinegar as oil, fill a pint jar halfway with the liquids. Depending on how spicy you want it, add as much of the ground chili pepper as you like.
2. Add the other ingredients and, with the lid securely fastened on the jar, shake the jar. Taste and adjust accordingly.
3. You can save this dressing for weeks in the refrigerator. It may solidify because of the oil, but will quickly turn back to liquid after it has been out of the fridge for a little while.

Refreshing Herbal Tea

You can use fresh or dried herbs for this tea. It's delicious served hot or cold.

Yield varies based on taste

2 parts lemon balm
1 part lemon verbena
1 part spearmint

Just follow the ratios listed and pack your tea ball with dried herbs, or let fresh ones steep loosely.

Hot Mediterranean Tea

You can use fresh or dried herbs for this tea, which means you can enjoy it year-round. This tea is best served hot, but you can try it cool on a hot summer day, if desired.

Yield varies based on taste

1 part summer savory
1 part marjoram
1 part rosemary

Follow the ratios listed and pack your tea ball with dried herbs, or let fresh ones steep loosely. Serve hot.

Lemon-Mint Sun Tea

This tea is great as a sun tea—just allow it to steep in the sun, covered, for a few hours. It is also good brewed as a traditional iced tea.

Yields 1 large pitcher

½ cup mint sprigs
1 lemon, quartered
Pitcher of clean water
Ice as needed

Add mint sprigs and lemon quarters to a pitcher of clean water, and cover with a cheesecloth or other light fabric. Place in the sun for several hours and then pour over ice, allowing the mint and lemons to remain loose as a pretty garnish.

COOK.

When making sun tea, it's best to use a glass or a ceramic pitcher. Some metals can react with the acidity in some herbs and fruit, affecting the flavor, and a plastic pitcher left in the sun tends to leach a bad taste into its contents.

Cucumber Basil Water

This refreshing, flavored water is a delicious accompaniment to any summertime meal, or on its own.

Yields 1 large pitcher

1 whole English cucumber or 2 pickling cucumbers
5 or 6 small sprigs of basil
Optional: 2 or 3 lemon wedges

1. Wash and cut ends off cucumber(s). Leave the peel on, and slice into moderately thin slices (not so thin as to be totally translucent).
2. Gently wash the basil so as not to bruise the leaves.
3. Separate the leaves from the stems. Do not cut.
4. Add cucumber and basil to water, add ice, and chill in the refrigerator for at least an hour before serving.
5. You can keep a pitcher in the fridge, adding more water when necessary, for a few days or until the basil starts to lose its freshness. Mint is also a good substitute for the basil.

Herb Pesto

A variation of the classic, more simple pesto, this version will make your mouth water. It's a great way to use lots of fresh herbs.

Yields 1 cup

½ cup packed fresh basil leaves
½ cup packed fresh parsley leaves
¼ cup packed fresh oregano leaves
3 garlic cloves
2 tablespoons grated Parmesan
2 tablespoons olive oil
2 teaspoons lemon juice
½ teaspoon salt
¼ teaspoon pepper
Optional: 1 ounce walnuts

1. Combine all the ingredients except for the oil, lemon juice, salt, and pepper. Use a food processor or blender to mix until finely chopped.
2. Gradually mix in the oil and lemon juice, and stir in the salt and pepper last.

Garden Herb Salad

This salad explodes with perfectly balanced flavors from your garden. The ideal taste of summertime greens, you'll find yourself dreaming of this salad year-round.

Yields 2 or 3 servings

2 cups lettuce leaves

2 cups spinach leaves

4 marjoram sprigs

2 tablespoons basil leaves

½ cup celery leaves

½ cup flat-leaf parsley leaves

Handful lemon verbena sprigs

1 cup purslane sprigs

Pinch of salt

Extra-virgin olive oil

Fresh lemon juice or apple cider vinegar

Any available herb blossoms

1. After washing, sorting, and drying all the lettuce and spinach leaves, tear or cut into bite-sized pieces.
2. Separate the marjoram leaves from stems, keeping leaves whole. Tear basil leaves into small pieces.
3. Keep the other herb leaves in their current condition.
4. Toss everything, with just a pinch of salt and a light application of oil.
5. Add lemon juice (or vinegar) to taste and toss in the blossoms.

PART 3

PRESERVE AND STORE

CHAPTER 5

WHERE TO STORE

To create delicious meals year-round, you'll need to preserve the fruits of your labor. But you don't want to grow ten pounds of carrots and have them spoil or can twenty Mason jars of Wild Strawberry Preserves (see recipe in Chapter 6) without having a place to store them. After all, storing food for year-round use is actually one of the most enjoyable parts of creating your own sustainable food system. In this chapter you will learn about the different types of spaces and structures for storing both whole foods and foods you've preserved, making sure that the food you've grown is ready to use when you need it.

THE ROOT CELLAR

The purpose of a root cellar is to store your fresh fruits and veggies so you can eat them during the winter months. If you are just starting to think about building a root cellar, or if you already have one, this chapter will help you learn how to get the most out of it. You will learn how to choose the best location and size, discover how to create the best conditions, and gain new knowledge about shelving and container options that will help you get the best possible results from your root cellar.

SIZE

The size of your root cellar will depend on how much food you want to store and what size root cellar you can build in a good location. A 10-foot by 12-foot root cellar will usually have plenty of space to store veggies, fruits, and both canned and dried goods for a family. Your requirements will vary, but if you are going to the expense of excavating or building a root cellar, you need to make sure it is large enough that you can grow into it as you gain more experience storing your foods.

In addition to being a basic size, your root cellar should ideally have at least two rooms, one colder than the other. Having two rooms allows you to regulate the humidity, temperature, and airflow, giving you the best storage conditions for a variety of foods. You will learn more about the storage requirements of specific vegetables later in this chapter.

Ideally you want your root cellar to be close to your garden so it is easy to put extra veggies directly into it when harvesting. You also want the root cellar to be easily accessible from your kitchen so you can get to your stored foods without any difficulty, especially on those cold winter days. If you live on flat ground, without a hillside available for excavation, you will most likely need to build an aboveground cellar. Otherwise, it is best to build your root cellar below ground.

A BELOWGROUND STRUCTURE

If you live on a site with a hillside or slope—one that can be easily excavated and that faces away from prevailing winds—you already have an ideal spot to build your root cellar. Using the earth as insulation is one of the best ways to protect your fruits and vegetables, and having three walls and the roof covered with soil is ideal. If at all possible, locate the entry door on the north side of the slope to help insulate the structure and provide minimal exposure to direct sunlight. You will want to avoid building in a low-lying area, and make sure your site has good drainage so that the cellar doesn't fill up with water.

Examine the soil content before you begin digging into your hillside. Soil that is rocky or hardpan clay may not allow for easy hand digging, which means that renting or buying excavation equipment may be necessary. Sandy soil can also provide difficulties, such as walls collapsing as you dig. There can be a variety of different types of soil on any property, and it may be necessary to consider a few potential sites before you settle on the right one.

Another thing to look out for when choosing a site for your underground root cellar is large trees. Tree roots can reach amazing distances and may cause a lot of problems during the excavation of the site. They can also invade the walls of your root cellar later on. If at all possible, avoid areas with large trees, and do not plant deep-rooted trees or shrubs nearby.

Walls and Doorways

A root cellar that has been dug into a hillside is an underground structure with one exposed wall and an access door. The wall can be made from a variety of materials such as wood, cement blocks, adobe, rammed earth, earthbags, or cob.

To create an access door for your underground cellar, first mark off a 32-inch space to serve as a rough opening for your doorway. Next, create the door frame out of 2-foot by 8-foot lumber boards. An economical option is to install a previously used door, often found at salvage yards, Habitat for Humanity ReStores, and garage sales.

Insulation

Depending on what material you choose to make your access wall and on the climate in your area, you may need to insulate your cellar. A wall made of wood will have to be insulated no matter what the climate, as wood alone will not keep the heat or cold from coming through. Two feet of insulation material, placed between the interior and exterior wall, is ideal for a wood-framed wall if you are using natural materials for insulation. A wall built with hollow cement blocks is easily insulated by filling in the hollow area between blocks with some common material such as sawdust, loose straw, or dry sand. Or, commercial insulation can be used. A wall made of adobe, rammed earth, or cob needs no additional insulation as it is thick enough and the material used functions as a natural insulator.

PRESERVE.

It may seem like common sense, but this bears repeating: Hot temperatures warm the earth and cold temperatures will freeze it. Both heat and cold affect the temperature inside your underground root cellar. All root cellars, whether they are built above or below the ground, require two air vents: one lower down on a wall to let in cool air and another higher up to allow the warm air to be released. Ventilation and good air circulation are required to keep the temperature regulated in any root cellar, and a ventilator may be necessary in certain root cellars.

Your access door will also need to be insulated. One way is to cover the inside of the door with standard home insulation. To do this, cut 2-foot by 4-foot boards long enough to make a frame around the inside of the door. Nail the wood to the door, then fill the 2-inch recess with insulation. Nail a piece of plywood to this frame to hold the insulation in place. A much easier way to provide insulation is to tack a heavy blanket or cloth to the inside of the door, although this may not be effective if you live in a very cold climate.

If your underground root cellar has more than one room, you can help regulate temperature and humidity by having well-insulated walls and doorways. Hanging blankets on interior walls and over doorways is one way to regulate temperature throughout the cellar and provide an extra measure of insulation for your fruits and veggies.

PRESERVE.
The roof will be made of soil in any underground root cellar. Interior framing may be supplied to support this dirt roof depending on the size of the cellar and the soil type, but that is all that is needed.

A PARTIAL UNDERGROUND STRUCTURE

If your location is not ideal for excavating a root cellar, you can build a partial underground structure by digging just 4 feet or so into the ground. This type of structure is common in colder parts of the country, in areas where the ground is flat and rocky, or where the water table is high and there is very poor drainage. The walls of a partial underground root cellar are usually made of masonry blocks and banked with soil on three sides.

First you will need to decide on the size of your root cellar. For example, if you want a structure 12 feet by 8 feet that will stay solid for years, you will need to dig an area 16 feet by 12 feet that sits 4 feet deep, with an entrance ramp that is 4 feet wide and slopes 6 feet. You want the hole to be larger than your structure so you have access to build your walls from all sides. Once it is built you can fill in the extra space on the outside of the wall with the dirt from the excavation; this will provide even more insulation for your root cellar. The entrance ramp is 6 feet long and angled, giving you an area to make steps leading down to the main door of your cellar. Make sure you have the space to accommodate the size structure you want to build before you start digging.

This type of structure traditionally has a hatchway door with a stairway leading down to a second doorway. The "double entrance" offers great insulation from the outside temperatures because of the air space between the two doors. The roof is typically made of two-by-fours and then protected with roof sheathing and plastic film, with dirt piled on top of everything. Vents are installed for good air circulation, and a drainage system is used to eliminate water and reduce humidity.

Two big advantages to the partial underground structure are that it is affordable and easy to build. If you utilize common materials from your own property or a local building-supply store, you can build this structure in your spare time.

AN ABOVEGROUND STRUCTURE

What if you want to store some of your own veggies for eating during the winter but do not have the type of property that will allow you to build an underground root cellar? An aboveground or partial aboveground structure is a viable option. You will have to build your structure above ground if you live on a flat property, which means making sure to provide proper insulation. Heat will penetrate the walls of your root cellar if the sun hits them, especially if they are made of concrete or wood, and this will warm the interior and cause the temperature to rise. Your stored fruits and veggies will dehydrate more quickly in tepid conditions. The room may freeze without proper insulation in the winter when the temperature gets below freezing, causing the fruits and vegetables to rot more quickly. Wiring your root cellar with electricity is another way to solve this problem.

Whichever method you choose, be sure to keep the temperature in your aboveground root cellar as consistent as possible. Completely underground root cellars usually stay at the ideal temperature for storing fruits and veggies due to the earth's natural insulation. However, you can still preserve successfully in an aboveground storage building so long as you build it in the right location and provide insulation and proper drainage. Constructing a solid aboveground structure begins with choosing the right materials for its walls.

Brick, Concrete Blocks, or Stone Walls

Brick, concrete blocks, and stone are some of the most common materials used in building the walls of the traditional aboveground root cellar. Usually the cost and availability of these materials are the most important factors in determining which of these products you choose. As you probably know, bricks come in a wide variety of sizes. They are typically small and therefore easy to work with, but because they are small you will need more product and your structure will take longer to construct. Concrete blocks are a good choice for making heavy-duty walls. They are usually cheaper than bricks and the construction will go much faster because of their larger size.

Building with stone or large rocks is often the cheapest option as these materials can often be found on your own property. The construction can be more challenging, however. You'll need a good eye, a strong back, and lots of patience to build sturdy walls from rocks that are all different shapes and sizes. However, building with stone can also give you a huge sense of accomplishment; not only will your structure have been built from materials gathered from your own land, it will have a handcrafted look and quality.

If you are new to building with rock and are not yet familiar with cutting the material, you will want to start with the flattest-edged rocks you can find for your first layer. Choose rocks that are similar in height to start building up your wall, continuing along the full length of the wall. Fill in all the joints between the rocks with mortar. When the first course is complete, spread mortar across the top and continue building another layer. If you run out of similar-sized rocks, find two that can be stacked to match the others. Stand back and look at the wall to make sure the joints are all staggered; if not, your wall has more of a chance of breaking.

Wooden Walls

Cedar is your best option if you decide to build your root cellar out of wood because cedar offers greater resistance to rot and insects. Your first step when building walls with wood is to create an insulation pocket. To do this, build two walls 2 feet apart, and fill this cavity with either traditional insulation or somewhat unconventional options such as straw, hay, or sawdust. It is important to cover the outside of your wood walls with a moisture-resistant material, especially if you are planning to pack soil against them.

Adobe Walls

Adobe is one of the first human-made building supplies, and was originally used where trees were scarce but there was an abundance of dirt and water. Making your own adobe takes a lot of time and work, but its considerable benefits make the investment worthwhile. Adobe provides natural insulation, consistent humidity, and fresh air exchange, all invaluable to your burgeoning root cellar.

PRESERVE.

Three of the most common roof types used for an aboveground cellar are sloped roofs, gable roofs, and flat roofs. The style of roof you choose will depend upon the overall appearance you want, the amount of money you want to spend, and the materials you have available. A flat or low-pitched roof is the most common style for a root cellar; however, a flat roof can be problematic if you live in a wet climate or where the snowfall is heavy. Whatever roofing style you choose, make sure it is properly built.

You will need molds to form your own bricks, and these can be made by hand using pieces of wooden two-by-fours that are cut and connected to the right size. To save time, build a mold that allows you to make multiple adobe bricks at once. The adobe mixture is made by combining soil, water, and cement. Begin by adding just enough water to the soil to make it slightly plastic, meaning you want the soil to be a muddy consistency but not watery so it will hold its shape. Next add the cement, followed by enough water to bring the mix to a molding consistency. Use a blade-type mixer to ensure proper mixing, or mix well by hand with a hoe.

Building Walls with Rammed Earth

Rammed-earth walls are made from earth and water. The ideal soil to use for these structures is a blend of small gravel, coarse or fine sand, and clay. The soil in the area of your root cellar can be tested to see if it is suitable for this use; if not, you can have better soil brought in. Cement can also be added to the soil to increase its strength and to help keep moisture out of the walls. Steel reinforcing bars are often used in the foundation and walls for added structural support.

The basic procedure for building a rammed-earth structure has not changed in the past two millennia. Suitable moist soil is compacted one layer at a time into a form that is constructed where the wall is to be. The form can be made out of two pieces of plywood with wood connecting them. The form is constructed to the width and height of the wall you are building. Once the form is full of soil and the last layer is compacted, the form is taken down and the process repeated for all remaining walls. The earth is compacted by hand or by machines.

PRESERVE.

To test your soil to determine if it will work well for building a rammed-earth structure, construct a small sample block and check it for strength and weather resistance. Spray the block with water from your garden hose at full force for an hour to see how it holds up. If necessary, modify your earth mix and make another test block.

The benefit to making rammed-earth walls is that earth is always readily available. In addition, it is unprocessed, low-cost, heat-storing, load-bearing, recyclable, and durable. A properly built rammed-earth root cellar gains free heat from the winter sun and stores that heat in its walls, preventing your food from freezing. During summer months, the walls absorb excess heat from the inside if the structure is properly shaded and ventilated, helping to keep the interior cool and allowing your food to stay fresh longer.

Building a Cob Structure

Cob is probably the oldest earth-building system and it also happens to be the simplest. A cob structure requires no framework, ramming, or additives, and is very easy to build. The word *cob* is an English term that means "mud building," so it's no surprise that a cob wall is made of a combination of sand, clay, straw, and water—all of which may be readily available right on your own property!

The cob recipe:

- 50–85 percent sand
- 50–15 percent clay
- Straw (add as much as you can until each piece is surrounded by the sand/clay mixture—the more clay in the mix, the more straw can be added)
- Water (add enough so the earth mixture holds together)

After you thoroughly mix these four ingredients, the stiff mud is piled to make a wall and formed using your own hands.

A cob structure typically takes several weeks to build. First, a stone foundation is laid and stiff mud is shoveled onto it and tamped down. Next, about 18 inches of material, know as a "lift of cob," is piled on top of this foundation, then left for two weeks to dry before the next "lift" is added. The walls are trimmed back as they dry using a paring iron, leaving them straight and plumb (meaning the wall is exactly vertical) and between 20 and 36 inches thick. Openings for a door and windows are built in by framing in lintels of stone or wood at appropriate heights as the walls are constructed.

Cob structures need protection from prolonged soaking. Building a strong foundation and roof and adding the additional protection of a coating of exterior plaster will ensure that your structure withstands the elements.

The benefits of cob walls are the same as with rammed earth; whether your cellar is built underground or partially underground, these types of walls help keep the temperature consistent and therefore prevent your stored items from getting too warm or too cold. The dirt floor in these structures makes it easier to maintain the proper humidity as well. Additionally, you'll be buying a minimal amount of materials if you decide to build cob walls, making them an inexpensive option. Plus, they can be fun to construct, especially if you enlist the help of your family, friends, and neighbors!

Use Earthbags

Another cost-effective alternative for building the walls of your aboveground root cellar is to use soil-filled sacks, also known as earthbags. This more flexible version of rammed earth is preferred in areas where the soil has very low clay content, where wood is scarce, or where the site is prone to floods, hurricanes, or wildfires. When properly built, earthbag walls are very strong.

When choosing which bag to use, you'll want to seek out bag material that's strong. The most commonly used bags are made from either burlap (hessian) or polypropylene. Burlap is more durable than polypropylene, and burlap is biodegradable because it is made from plant fibers. Polypropylene bags are made of woven plastic and are photodegradable, meaning that they will deteriorate if exposed to ultraviolet rays from the sun. Recycled seed or feed sacks are good choices for either of these materials.

First, fill the bags with subsoil, removing any organic matter and topsoil. You can also fill the bags with gravel, which may be handy if you are using gravel for the foundation. Then stack the bags layer upon layer, in a staggered pattern to prevent rain from seeping into the wall.

UNCONVENTIONAL STORAGE SPACES

Even if you live in a rental home or an apartment, or do not have any traditional space to build a root cellar, the average home usually has a few spots that would make great unconventional root cellars. When looking around your home, try to find areas that have good storage conditions—a cold, damp space for root vegetables like potatoes and carrots; a warm dry spot for storing squash; and a cool, dry area for your garlic and onions.

SPACES THROUGHOUT YOUR HOME

An unheated room such as a spare bedroom, an unused bath, or a closet that doesn't see much use are all great candidates for your cold-storage area. Close the door to the space, put in a thermometer, and record the temperature. If it is cool

(32°F–40°F) and moist (80–90 percent relative humidity), you have found a great place to store your root veggies. If the area is cool (32°F–50°F) but dry (60–70 percent relative humidity), then it is the place to store your garlic and onions.

PRESERVE.

Before storing beets, carrots, rutabagas, and other root vegetables, make sure the leafy green tops are removed. Tops that are not removed will quickly deplete the nutrients found in the root vegetable. Leave an inch or so of stem so the peel of the vegetable is not broken. This practice will also help to keep your vegetables crisp longer.

An unheated attic is usually easily accessible and often has the ideal conditions for storing vegetables such as squash and green tomatoes. A warm attic is also a good spot for drying herbs, nuts, and beans. Make sure your vegetables, herbs, and nuts are in perfect condition before placing them in boxes or hanging them in your attic. Some vegetables, such as tomatoes, will have to be checked regularly as they can ripen fairly quickly. Others, such as good quality squash, can last up to six months when stored properly. Because most attics are unheated, you'll occasionally need to open the door to let in a little heat. Another option for storing your squash is under your bed—an area that is normally warm, dry, and unused.

Wall space along stairwells up to your attic or down to your basement can hold small containers or baskets of apples, onions, or garlic. On the floor under your kitchen table may even be a spot to store a few of those green tomatoes so they can easily be checked and pulled out to eat when ripe.

PORCHES AND BASEMENTS

Your living space may not be big enough or convenient if you have a large amount of food to store. In this case, an enclosed porch or basement may offer the perfect solution.

An enclosed porch is usually a dry, unheated room; in other words, it is a great place for food storage. It would be a good spot to store potatoes for a short time, while onions, garlic, nuts, canned goods, and dried goods could be stored there for a long time. Just make sure that they do not get direct sunlight and that the area does not freeze.

There are often crawlspaces under porches or patios that offer great storage conditions—dark, cold, and damp. One concern with a crawlspace is it is usually not insulated, meaning your food will need to be protected from freezing. If you live in an extremely cold climate, insulate with straw, sawdust, or leaves to help prevent severe fluctuations in temperature. A crawlspace can be difficult to get in and out of, so make sure you know exactly what you are putting into the area. A diagram that shows where items are placed can be helpful when you are searching for a particular vegetable in the middle of the winter.

Most basements have unused areas that are cool, dry, and easily accessible, making them another ideal area for use as an unconventional root cellar. You will want the basement to be well ventilated and to maintain a temperature between 50°F and 60°F. This is a good area for ripening tomatoes as well as for storing squash, potatoes, carrots, and onions over a short period of time. If you can, build an insulated room away from your furnace to help these items keep longer. Make sure any storage containers are set off the floor. The floor may also need to be dampened occasionally to keep the humidity high enough so the veggies do not shrivel. Damp sawdust scattered on the basement floor will also help.

Basement window wells can also be used for cold storage, and windows can be opened to provide extra cooling if needed. These areas are usually fairly small, but have the distinct advantage of being well off the floor. Place your veggies in a box or container in the window well, scattering some wood shavings around the outside of the container for extra insulation. It's important to make sure you are not storing food items near your furnace when using your basement, as this area is often too warm to successfully store any fruits or veggies. On the other hand, a furnace room with sturdy shelves offers a great place to store your jars of canned foods and preserves.

OUTBUILDINGS

If your home does not have a porch or basement, outbuildings such as a garage or gardening shed can be used to store your fruits and veggies. A garden shed can be used for hanging dried herbs, garlic, or onions, and the garage is great for storing root vegetables. Many garages are unheated, but most are insulated and therefore provide an ideal freeze-resistant spot to store a few boxes of potatoes, carrots, or beets.

The climate you live in will determine how long you can store items in an unheated garden shed. If you live in an area that gets long periods of below-freezing temperatures, your fruits and vegetables will probably freeze if stored there. A structure made of cement or rammed earth, as discussed in the previous section about aboveground root cellars, will be better able to support your food in these extreme conditions.

If the only space you have available is an unheated shed, you can pack your fruits and vegetables into containers with wood shavings, sawdust, straw, or peat moss between the layers to help insulate the food from extreme cold. Hanging blankets on the shed walls will add further insulation from the damaging cold. If your shed floor is made of dirt, digging a pit right under the shed will help to insulate your stored items even more. Your potatoes and carrots may not last all winter long in these conditions, but you will be able to enjoy them for a few months at least, so give it a try!

ROOT-CELLAR CONDITIONS

Cool temperatures, high humidity, good air circulation, and proper ventilation are essential to having a well-functioning root cellar, no matter what type of root cellar you plan to use: underground, aboveground, or even your own basement. You want to be able to enjoy the produce you reaped from your garden in the delicious dishes included throughout this book, so you'll want to make sure your root cellar is up to par. If you lose more than 30 percent of your crop to spoilage each season, you will have to figure out which of these conditions are not being met.

TEMPERATURE

The optimum temperature for your root cellar is between 32°F and 40°F. This fairly cool temperature helps to slow the release of ethylene gas from certain vegetables and will also slow the growth of microorganisms that cause foods to decompose. If the temperature gets too warm, the food will rot or get moldy; too cool a temperature and the food will freeze, causing it to become soft and mushy after it thaws again. Extreme temperatures will cause the food in your root cellar to deteriorate faster, so it is important to make sure you insulate well and regulate the temperature.

The temperature in a root cellar is never uniform, and knowing which areas are colder or warmer will enable you to store your produce in the proper areas. You will need at least two thermometers to regulate the temperature inside your root cellar. Place one in the coldest part of the cellar and one on the outside of your structure, and closely monitor each area. Regulate the inside temperature by opening doors and windows, and by opening or closing ventilation pipes.

HUMIDITY

The optimum relative humidity in a root cellar is between 85 and 95 percent, and every root cellar should have a hygrometer to properly regulate the humidity. Too much moisture and your food will rot and deteriorate more quickly; too little and your food will shrivel up, leaving nothing for you to eat.

A damp dirt floor will give you the best results for achieving the ideal humidity in your root cellar. A concrete floor will also work, but it will tend to lower the humidity in the cellar and therefore needs more regulating to get the best results.

Here are some easy ways to add moisture to your root cellar:

- Sprinkle the floor with water, especially a few days before you start bringing in the freshly harvested veggies.
- Leave large pans of water near the intake air vents.
- Cover the floors with wet materials such as damp straw or sawdust.
- Shovel some snow into the root cellar to cool and humidify the area.
- Pack vegetables in damp sawdust or peat moss.

Too much humidity can be just as damaging to the food stored in your root cellar as too little. Cold air does not hold as much moisture as warm air, so moisture will collect on the roof or shelves and cause condensation if the cellar has too high a humidity content. Keeping the humidity regulated so there is no condensation is your best practice for preserving your food. If condensation does appear, make sure no water is dripping directly onto your vegetables or fruits.

VENTILATION AND AIR CIRCULATION

Make sure your root cellar is equipped with one vent allowing air to flow in and another vent allowing air to be released. Keep in mind that it is easiest to put these vents in when building your root cellar. Ideally you will want the intake vent to be low and the outflow vent to be placed higher up; cool air will be able to enter the cellar, and as warm air rises it will be released through the outlet vent. A mesh cover placed over each vent will prevent rodents from getting in.

The most practical item to use as a vent is a 6-inch water or sewer pipe wrapped in duct insulation. Attaching an elbow at the end exposed to the outside will help keep the temperature consistent. Do not glue this elbow; you want to make sure it is free to turn away from the prevailing wind.

The vents allow both the temperature to adjust and the air in the root cellar to circulate freely. In extremely cold or extremely warm climates, you have the option of blocking the intake vent to prevent intense temperatures from entering. Make sure you open it regularly to allow the air to circulate as this is a critical factor in minimizing airborne mold. One way of maximizing airflow is to make sure your shelves sit a few inches away from the walls. Another is to store containers of food and jars of preserves with some space between each.

SHELVING

In addition to keeping your cellar more organized, shelving helps keep your veggies fresher. Fruits and vegetables put directly onto the floor of a root cellar will rot and deteriorate more quickly because they will either become too moist or get too cold. Shelving allows the air to circulate freely around your stored foods. Some foods, such as cabbage, onions, and apples, give off ethylene gases, and so you'll want to make sure these foods are put in an out-of-the-way corner or on the topmost shelf to prevent them from affecting other produce.

There are many shelving options available for use in your root cellar. You can build sturdy wood shelves, use metal or plastic shelving, make use of recycled items such as old cabinetry or cement blocks with wood slats laid across them, or install any other item that will stack or can be easily hung on a wall. Make sure your shelves are the right height to allow your containers to get air circulation around the top as well as the sides. Your shelves should be sturdily built to hold heavy items. Shelves that use slats are one of the better options because they will support those heavier items and allow for extra air circulation around your containers and jars. You will also want your shelves to be easily removed so they can be cleaned at least once a year.

PITS AND TRENCHES

If you have a lot of root vegetables such as potatoes, carrots, beets, and rutabagas to store and do not have a root cellar or other indoor space available, a pit or trench might be another option to utilize. A pit or trench can come close to creating the same conditions you would find in a root cellar—cool temperatures but not freezing, humid but not too damp, some type of ventilation, and protection from critters of all kinds.

A word of warning: a pit or trench is not a "for sure" thing. The spot you choose may look dry and suitable in September, but by January it may be a soggy mess, and mice and other creatures will have found their way into your food. Your climate is a big factor when using pits and trenches; if you live in an extremely cold climate, the food will easily freeze no matter how much straw or leaves you use for insulation.

Pits should be small, and it is best to store no more than a week's worth of food in each pit, so that you empty it all at one time and transfer its contents inside to the refrigerator for the week's meals. A pit is great for storing potatoes, carrots, parsnips, Brussels sprouts, turnips, rutabagas, cabbages, and apples.

To create your pit, dig a hole 1 foot deep and 3 feet square in an area that you know has good drainage. Line the hole with 3 to 4 inches of straw, hay, or leaves. Gently place the vegetables into the pit in a pyramid shape—do not just throw the veggies in as they can be easily bruised or broken. Cover them with a foot of straw or leaves, and then cover the straw with soil. If you think mice or other critters will be a problem, place hardware cloth or a screen over the vegetables before covering them with the straw and soil.

You now need to work on ventilating your pit. Loosely layered straw and hay might provide sufficient ventilation, or you can use a metal can or pipe that has both ends open. Place the can on top of the pile of vegetables, making sure the top of it is not covered with the straw or soil mulch. It is important to cover the top of the can with mesh to help prevent mice, birds, and other animals from using it as a doorway to their next meal.

Trenches are used to store leafy vegetables such as cabbages, celery, Brussels sprouts, and Chinese cabbages. Like a pit, a trench will not keep your veggies from freezing if you live in a cold climate. To build your trench, dig a channel 1 foot deep (or more depending on what you are storing), 2 feet wide, and whatever length you may need. If the soil is loose, you may want to prop up the sides with boards.

Dig up the plants (including their roots) that you want to winter over, then transplant them closely together in the trench. Make sure the roots are well covered with soil and that the top of the plant is not higher than the height of the trench. Once transplanted, water the plant roots, making sure the leaves do not get wet. Leave the plants for a few hours to settle and then place a board over the trench, covering the vegetables. Cover the board with a foot of straw, hay, or leaves and place a piece of plastic or a tarp over everything. To remove the plants, open one end of the trench, remove what you need, and then close it up again.

Burying a barrel is another way to store some veggies; a wooden barrel covered with straw would work well. You can use any type of barrel except plastic, and make sure there was nothing in the barrel previously that could poison your food. Stay completely away from anything that may have contained any pesticides or other toxic substances.

Dig a hole deep enough to contain the barrel. Make sure about 2 inches of the barrel are left above ground, keeping in mind that you'll be placing a few inches of rocks or pea gravel in the bottom of the hole for the barrel to sit on. Cut a hole in the bottom of the barrel for drainage, making sure you cover it with mesh or screen to keep out any critters. Place your veggies into the barrel, layering with straw every foot or so. Cover the filled barrel with at least 3 to 4 inches of straw that extends several inches larger in diameter than the barrel. You may want to put in a ventilation pipe for better circulation, again making sure you cover the top of the pipe with fine-mesh screen.

VEGETABLE STORAGE

Keep in mind that all vegetables have different storage characteristics. Some cannot be stored; others will last for several months with only a little care or attention. Learning which vegetables will store best in your conditions is often based on trial and error. Every vegetable plant has different growing circumstances that will either let it store better or cause it to deteriorate more quickly, and the conditions in your root cellar or storage area may vary from year to year as well. This means you may have to deal with different successes or problems every season, but having fresh veggies to eat during the winter months is well worth the effort.

Now that you know where to store your fruits, veggies, and herbs, it's time to take a look at how to can and preserve them so you can enjoy preparing your favorite rustic recipes whenever you desire.

CHAPTER 6

CAN AND PRESERVE

To create delicious, rustic meals for you family year-round, preserving the food from your garden is a necessary part of sustainability. After all, what better way to remember and appreciate the hard work and fun of summertime come winter than by sharing a meal of homegrown food with the loved ones who helped to produce it, preserve it, and cook it? In this chapter, you'll find info on how to can, dry, freeze, ferment, and pickle the fruits, veggies, and herbs you worked so hard to grow. You'll also find a list of the best way to preserve many of the fruits, vegetables, and herbs discussed in Part 2 as well as a variety of delicious recipes including Blueberry Chutney, Caramelized Red Onion Relish, and Pickled Cherry Tomatoes that you can enjoy right out of the jar, freezer, or oven.

DETERMINING THE BEST PRESERVATION METHOD

When preserving food, it is important to know that there is usually a best way to preserve each food, and to also be aware that some foods can be preserved in multiple ways. With the basic objective of handling and keeping food so that it maintains quality flavors, textures, and colors while avoiding the spoilage and bacterial growth that cause illness, you want to choose the method of preservation that balances what is best for the food with what is conducive to your storage and preservation system.

For example, many vegetables are best and easily frozen, but if you do not have access to freezer space, then you will have to consider other preservation methods. In some cases, employing a few different preservation techniques for the same vegetable is a good idea because it puts less strain on a single storage component (that is, less food in your freezer or fewer cans in your pantry). Foods preserved in different ways can be cooked differently, adding a fun variety to the recipes found throughout this chapter and book.

CANNING

Canning begins with good food and sterile jars. It's very important that the storage containers used in canning are properly cleaned to kill bacteria. Additionally, canning includes hot-water baths (for high-acid items) and pressure-cooking (for low-acid items) to create a vacuum and kill off any lingering, potentially harmful microbes, specifically botulism, which has no odor or taste and is potentially deadly.

Many people have rediscovered the art of canning because it offers flexibility and variety to an at-home food system. Canned food can last a long time, can be stored in lots of places, and won't take up room in a freezer. If you're nervous about canning food, the processes used today are very safe when you follow the directions carefully and understand what you're doing.

CANNING EQUIPMENT

The most important piece of equipment is the canner itself, and you want to give yourself a few options by having a large pressure cooker and a hot-water-bath canner, which is really nothing more than a large pot.

Hot-water-bath canners are made of aluminum or porcelain-covered steel. They have removable perforated racks and fitted lids. You need a hot-water canner that is deep enough to submerge the jars you're using—at least 1 inch of briskly boiling water must cover the tops of jars during processing. Some boiling-water canners do not have flat bottoms, which are essential for use on an electric range. Either a flat or ridged bottom can be used on a gas burner. To ensure uniform processing of all jars with an electric range, the diameter of the canner should be no more than 4 inches wider than the element on which it is heated. Look for one that has a rack for the jars so they don't clank together during boiling. Some home preservers use a large stockpot and homemade rack system, but it is also very easy to find affordable hot-water-bath canning kits starting at around $30.

PRESERVE

Only Mason jars are safe for canning. Commercial jars such as mayonnaise and peanut butter jars are designed for one-time use only; they may crack or shatter in either a water-bath canner or a pressure cooker. Use canning jars in sizes suitable for the product and your family's needs. Canning jars generally are sold in half-pint, pint, and quart sizes with wide and regular mouths. Wide-mouth jars are convenient for packing such foods as whole tomatoes and peach halves. Quart jars are convenient for vegetables and fruits if your family has four or more members.

The simple rule of thumb is that all high-acid foods go into a hot-water-bath canner and everything else must be processed in a pressure cooker. High-acid foods include all fruit products (jams, jellies, preserves, conserves, fruit butters, and marmalades) and anything pickled with vinegar such as pickles, relishes, and vinegar-based sauces. The hot-water bath increases the temperature in the canning jar enough to kill bacteria and it also pushes out air bubbles as the content expands. As the jars cool, the air pressure creates a seal that makes the lid pop.

Some additional, basic canning equipment that you should have on hand includes the following. You probably already own some of the items on this list, so check your home before you buy.

- Canning jars—pints, quarts, and Mason jelly jars
- Lids and rings (also called screw bands)
- Canning funnel
- Colander and/or large strainer
- Squeezer or juicer
- Food mill, food processor, and/or blender
- Canning-jar lifter and lid wand
- Stirrer for getting air bubbles out of jars
- Kitchen timer
- Cheesecloth for making spice balls or large tea balls
- Pickling or canning salt, Fruit-Fresh, powdered and liquid pectin, and Clear Jel
- Disposable rubber gloves
- Long-handled jar scrubber
- Optional: kitchen scale
- Optional: jelly bags

PREPARATION

Before you start canning, read your recipe at least twice and get your ingredients and supplies together. Prepare your workspace to allow for ample working room, and remember, canning projects require your uninterrupted attention from start to finish.

Determine how many jars your recipe calls for and examine these jars carefully, making certain there are no cracks or chips. You may put them through a sterilizing cycle in a dishwasher if you have one. Otherwise, use a bottle brush to scrub them inside and out, rinse them in hot water, and sterilize them in a stockpot or water-bath canner. Meanwhile, your lids should be placed in a bowl of hot water to soften the rubber sealing compound.

COOK.

You cannot use just any recipe when canning food. Recipes specific to canning should be used, and only ones that have been tested to guarantee food safety. This is particularly true when canning foods that combine ingredients with different pH levels. Most recipes that you find that are specific to canning have been tested, but it is still a good idea to use only recipes from reputable sources, like those found in this chapter. If you're sharing recipes with any friends, be sure to ask where they got their recipes!

PROCESSING

After following your recipe, fill your jars with the prepared food. Although the process is basically the same, the details will vary slightly depending on whether you are using a hot-water bath or a pressure cooker. If you are using the hot-water-bath method, leave ¼ inch of headroom at the top of your jar. If you use a pressure cooker, leave 1 inch of headroom at the top.

For a hot-water bath, jars are placed on a rack and covered with 1–2 inches of boiling water. Put a lid on the pot and begin timing when water is boiling. Remove jars with a jar lifter and place them on a towel-covered counter to cool. Leave undisturbed for twelve to twenty-four hours. Check the seals and remove the screw bands.

When using a pressure cooker, jars are placed on a rack and boiling water is added according to the manufacturer's instructions, usually several inches. Lock the lid securely into place. Leave weight off the vent pipe or open the petcock (exhaust vent), and exhaust steam for ten minutes. Place weight back onto vent pipe or close petcock. Canner should start to pressurize in five to ten minutes. Once the canner has reached the required amount of pressure, start the cooking timer.

After cooking, allow the canner to come down to zero pounds on its own. Do not try to speed up this process by removing weight or opening the petcock, as it may cause jars to crack and/or lose liquid. Do not put the canner into cold water to hasten the process. Let jars sit in the canner for five to ten minutes to allow them to cool down. Remove jars with a jar lifter and place them on a towel-covered counter to cool. Leave undisturbed for twelve to twenty-four hours. Check the seals and remove the screw bands (rings).

To check the seals on cooled jars, press your thumb in the middle of the lid. If the lid seems to give and come back up, the jar isn't sealed. If you're not sure, tap the lid with a knife in the same place. It should sound like a bell; a muffled sound means the jar isn't sealed right. Finally, there's the visual test; the surface of the lid should be concave.

What happens if your jar doesn't seal properly? All is not lost! You can put the jar in the refrigerator and use it soon.

AFTER PROCESSING

Wash off all your sealed jars, label them, and move them into a suitable storage place. To prevent spoiling, keep your jars away from places that are too hot or damp, and don't expose them to bright light. Use your canned goods within one year unless otherwise specified by the recipe. Either write expiration dates on your jars to remind you how long they will remain good, or write the canning date on the jar and figure the time accordingly.

When you use your canned goods, always check for signs of spoilage. The most obvious sign is the loss of a vacuum seal on the jar and mold growing inside. Other indicators include gas bubbles, odd coloring, and foul smells. When you open a can for use, you should hear the lid "pop" as the seal is broken. If there is no vacuum seal and the lid does not pop as the seal is broken, it means the lid did not seal properly. In that case, you must dispose of all food contents immediately. Never test suspect food—throw it out!

PRESERVE.

To make it easier to keep track of the cans you have in your pantry, post a piece of graph paper on the door or wall. Each time you place jars in the pantry, mark the appropriate number of squares next to it on the list—one square per jar. Each time you take a jar out, cross that square off with an X. This way you can easily tell how many jars of an item you have in stock.

DRYING

Drying was one of the first preserving methods ever used, probably because of its simplicity. It's also a very effective way of preserving many foods because it decreases water, therefore thwarting or slowing any unhealthy organism's growth. Although you can get commercial equipment designed for drying, there are items already in your home that will fit the bill nicely. An additional advantage to drying is that food has a long shelf life when it's dried properly. Without water content, food packs neatly onto cupboard shelves or storage areas. Drying is best suited to meats, fruits, herbs, mushrooms, and grains.

PRESERVE.

A large-scale food-drying effort occurred at the beginning of World War I when food was needed to feed the troops. The Great Depression in the 1930s led to more households using dry foods, as canning equipment was expensive and not readily available. During World War II, vegetable-dehydrating factories opened all across the United States as dried food had the advantage of being lightweight, compact, easy to transport, and enjoyed a long shelf life.

DRYING METHODS

Temperature variations and humidity will affect the drying process, specifically how long it will take. Pay attention to these things so that you can adjust your drying method accordingly. Food can be dried in a variety of ways.

Herbs and flowers are the most common air-dried foods. Remember to harvest in the morning and, if you're hanging the plants, don't bundle too many together—about six stems to a bundle is good. Hang them upside down from a string in a dry, warm spot with a paper lunch bag draped loosely over the bundle to keep it free of dust and to protect against sunlight. Use a toothpick to make holes in the bag to allow air to circulate. The plant matter should be dry in fourteen days.

Depending on what you're drying, another method is to remove the flower petals or herb leaves from the stem and lay them on a screen. It's very important that the screening material be clean and that the plant pieces don't touch each other. Place a piece of cheesecloth (or a large paper bag with pinholes in it) over the top of the screen. Again, this protects the flowers and herbs from airborne dust and dirt. Keep the trays out of the sunlight and in a cool, dry area. As with hanging, it takes about two weeks to dry the plant matter.

Oven Drying

Oven drying can be costly because your oven is not designed to maintain a low heat efficiently. Using your oven to dry food is only recommended if you won't be drying enough food to warrant buying a dehydrator. Because you're leaving food on low heat for many hours, if you regularly use your oven to dry food, the resulting energy costs will end up being more than the cost of a new dehydrator.

On the other hand, oven drying is very simple. Simply preheat your oven to 140°F, and pre-prepare your food according to instructions. Most oven trays hold up to 2 pounds of food. Unless you have a very large oven, it's suggested that you dry no more than three trays at a time, shifting their position and turning the food every thirty minutes for best results. Finally, try to keep the door of the oven open about 2 inches throughout this time. This improves air circulation and decreases the amount of heat you lose when you circulate the drying items.

Food Dehydrator

Using a commercial electric dehydrator takes half the time of drying in an oven, making it perfect for the energy-conscious consumer. These devices are created specifically to maintain air circulation, sustain even heating, and safeguard nutritional value. Fruits, herbs, and meats are good candidates for the dehydrator.

The market for dehydrators has grown, which means you can find some great optional features. You can pay more than $300 for a stainless-steel dehumidifier with 16 cubic square feet of interior space, but most home preservers don't need anything quite so elaborate. If you spend between $60 and $75, you can easily get a good quality machine.

When you decide to purchase a dehydrator, it's best to buy the type that heats and fans from the sides, as opposed to the bottom. Drying from the sides produces better results when you want to preserve a variety of items at one time because it doesn't allow the flavors to mix.

FRESHNESS, ATTENTIVENESS, AND AIRFLOW

In drying, "fresh is best" is your mantra. The sooner you begin drying items after they've been harvested, the happier you'll be with the results. This is also one of the few times in cooking when you'll hear "faster is better." When you carefully and quickly dry food once it is harvested, it helps create a continuity of texture and ensures that the center of the item doesn't retain moisture. Nonetheless, most drying techniques do take a little while, so allow for the time in your schedule. If you have to stop in the middle of drying something, you're opening the door for microbial growth.

FREEZING

Freezing and refrigeration are the most common types of home food preservation. Whereas refrigeration slows bacterial action, freezing comes close to totally stopping microbes' development. This happens because the water in frozen food turns to ice, in which bacteria cannot continue to grow. Enzyme activity, on the other hand, isn't completely deterred by freezing, which is why many vegetables are blanched before being packaged. Except for eggs in the shell, nearly all raw foods can be frozen, or frozen after blanching or cooking.

If you're ever in doubt about how to best prepare an item for freezing, the National Center for Home Food Preservation (*www.uga.edu/nchfp*) is a great online resource. It offers tips on how to freeze various items ranging from pie and prepared food to oysters and artichokes.

EQUIPMENT

Once you're ready to begin freezing food, assemble all the items you need. For example, if you're freezing fruit, you'll want a clean cutting board, a sharp knife, and your choice of storage containers. If you're doing any preparation of the fruit before freezing it, you'll also need cooking pans. Stainless steel is highly recommended; galvanized pans may give off zinc when fruit is left in them because of the fruit's acid content.

If it's in your budget, a vacuum sealer is another great piece of equipment. Vacuum sealers come in a variety of sizes with a similar variety of bags that are perfect for people who like freezing and drying methods. They're fairly cost-effective when compared to freezer bags or plastic containers, and they eliminate the excess air that contributes to ice crystals. Keeping air and ice crystals out of your frozen food packages will greatly enhance your food quality for longer periods of time, helping to prevent freezer burn. A third item that you shouldn't be without is a freezer-proof label system that includes the packaging date as well as the name of the item.

LOCATION AND SPACE

Consider your space constraints. Where are you going to put the freezer? Does that space have a suitable electrical outlet? Many new appliances require a 220-volt electrical line for them to run effectively. Placing the freezer in a cooler area of your home will help keep the cost of operating your freezer down. Once you've found a spot, measure it. That measurement will tell you quickly if you can get an upright or chest freezer.

An upright is very easy to access, especially if someone in your family has back problems. When you open the door, a fast visual survey will tell you what's inside. Uprights also typically offer conveniences such as auto defrost and ice makers. Chest freezers, by comparison, hold more food. They allow you to store oddly shaped items inside, and the internal temperature varies less than in an upright. On the down side, you may forget what's in the bottom, and you'll have to manually defrost these foods. However, foods will last longer in a chest freezer that requires manual defrosting—auto defrost features suck the humidity out of frozen foods and thus tend to promote freezer burn.

THE FREEZING PROCESS

The first step in freezing is keeping those items cold until you're ready to prepare them. This is very important with meat, but it also makes a difference in how fruits and vegetables come out of the freezer.

Next, you want to blanch your produce. Blanching has several benefits. It stops enzyme action that decreases vegetables' textural quality, flavor, and color, and it cleans off any lingering dirt. To blanch vegetables, fill a pan with water and bring it to a rolling boil. Add the vegetables and make sure they're immersed. Follow the blanching time recommended in the recipe and then turn the vegetables into a bowl of ice. Icing enables vegetables to retain their vitamins and firmness.

If there's no specific blanching time or technique provided in your preserving recipe, the following brief overview will get you started. Remember to move your produce into an ice bath immediately after blanching until it's totally cooled.

- **Asparagus:** Remove the tough ends from the asparagus. Depending on the storage container, you may need to cut the stems in half. If your stalks are thin, they'll only need 2 minutes of blanching; thick stalks require twice as much.
- **Beans (green or wax):** Remove any tips. Leave the beans whole and blanch them for 3 minutes.

- **Broccoli:** Break off the pieces from the central core and clean well (a spray nozzle at the sink works very well). Soak in a gallon of saltwater (3–4 teaspoons salt) for 30 minutes. Pour off the saltwater. Rinse and blanch for 3 minutes.
- **Brussels sprouts:** Clean off outer leaves, then soak the sprouts in cold saltwater for 30 minutes. Drain and blanch for 4 minutes.
- **Cabbage:** Remove the outer leaves. Shred the cabbage and blanch for just over 1 minute and leave in the water for another 30 seconds before icing.
- **Carrots:** Clean the skins, then slice into ¼-inch pieces. Blanch for 3 minutes. Whole baby carrots need 5 minutes of blanching.
- **Cauliflower:** Break off the pieces from the central core and clean well (a spray nozzle at the sink works very well). Soak in a gallon of saltwater (3–4 teaspoons salt) for 30 minutes. Pour off the saltwater. Rinse and blanch for 3 minutes.
- **Corn:** Rinse, remove from the cob, and blanch for 5 minutes.
- **Greens (including spinach):** Rinse. Remove any leaves that have spots or other damage. Blanch for 3 minutes.
- **Mushrooms (small):** These can be frozen whole. (They can also be dried.) Toss with a little fresh lemon juice and blanch for 4 minutes.
- **Peas:** Blanch out of the husk for 90 seconds.
- **Peas in the pod:** Trim the ends and remove strings. Blanch for 1–2 minutes, depending on the size of the pod.
- **Peppers:** Slice open and remove the seeds. Cut into desired size and blanch for 2 minutes.
- **Potatoes:** Wash and scrub thoroughly. Remove the peel and blanch for 4 minutes.
- **Tomatoes:** To easily peel the skins, use a straining spoon and dip the tomatoes in boiling water for 30 seconds. Peel and remove the core. These can be stored whole or diced to desired size.
- **Zucchini and squash:** Peel. Cut into ½-inch slices and blanch for 3 minutes.

PACKING FROZEN FOODS

It's always a good idea to use bags and containers that are rated for freezing, and to provide an extra layer of protection with aluminum foil or freezer wrap, particularly on meats. It's especially important to keep as much air out of the containers as possible, thus the benefit of using a vacuum sealer. Avoid using waxed cartons; they don't retain the food's quality very well and defrosted food often becomes limp and unstable for handling. Your packaging materials should also be leak-proof and oil resistant, and all packing materials should be able to withstand freezing.

Another consideration with your containers is size. Think about how many people you plan to serve and choose freezing containers accordingly. If you're going to put several servings in one large container, separate them with a piece of aluminum foil or plastic wrap so you can take out one at a time fairly easily.

Most important, remember to label and date everything. This will help you gauge what should be eaten first so it retains the greatest quality.

PRESERVE.

Glass containers can be used in the freezer, but you need to be very careful if you choose to do this! Test your containers first by putting a jar into a plastic bag and placing it in the freezer overnight. This way the pieces will be contained in the bag if it shatters. Even after testing, it is advisable to freeze glass jars in plastic bags, as accidents may happen.

SAFE STORAGE TIMES AND DEFROSTING

Frozen food can be kept nearly indefinitely at 0°F or colder. Nonetheless, the longer the food stays frozen, the more nutrients you lose and the greater the likelihood that ice crystals or freezer burn will form and decrease the overall color, taste, or textural quality of the product. One great way to deter this is by rotating foods so that the most recent entry to the freezer goes in the back.

After all the hard work that went into raising and storing your food, you'll want to defrost the food properly. The first rule of defrosting is that you don't leave anything at room temperature for hours at a time. Instead, choose one of these three tried-and-true ways to safely defrost your food.

1. **Leave the food in your refrigerator to defrost.** This takes a while, and it's wise to put some paper towels down or a platter underneath the item to catch any water or juices that run out during defrosting.
2. **Put the food in a cold-water bath; do not use warm or hot water.** Keep the item in the wrapper or container, and if need be put it in an additional resealable bag for protection. It's recommended that you refresh the water every 30 minutes until the item is defrosted.

3. **Use the defrost setting on your microwave.** Microwave powers vary greatly from machine to machine, so watch carefully to make sure your food isn't being partially cooked because that can give your food a rubbery texture.

PICKLING

There are four basic types of pickles. The first is fresh pack, which is blissfully simple to prepare. Second are fruit pickles that are prepared with a sugar-vinegar syrup. Third includes chutney and relish, and finally, the most popular is salt-cured or brined pickles. No matter what type of pickle you intend to preserve, always start with firm fruits or vegetables, fresh spices, and clean water. If you're harvesting your own fruits and vegetables, do so early in the morning and refrigerate them immediately before preparing all your pickling equipment. This is also true of store-bought items. Heat makes pickled items softer.

EQUIPMENT

One of the great beauties of pickling is that it doesn't require a lot of fancy equipment. Stainless steel and glass are ideal for pickling projects. Aluminum, enamel, and iron pots or tools aren't recommended because of the brine's natural acidity; when the acid reacts with those bases it changes the flavor of the resulting food. The following list includes some of the items you'll want for pickling:

- Paring knife
- Vegetable peeler
- Stone jar or crockery for fermenting (Note: You will need a plate or other cover that fits inside your fermenting jar. This holds the pickles beneath the brine. Kitchen plates work well.)
- Large bowl, plastic zip-top bag, or plastic food container (these may substitute for the stone jar or crockery as a fermenting vessel)
- Pots large enough for simmering the brine and spices
- Ladle
- Funnel
- Measuring tools
- Storage jars or containers
- Hot-water canner (if you're planning to put up the pickles)

EMBRACING BRINE

Brining has become a very popular method in cooking, not just for pickling but also for marinating. For example, some people who love deep-fried turkey swear by an herb-laced brine as one method for making a truly flavorful bird. The longer an item remains in a brine, the more it changes the taste and texture of the food.

Brining is very easy and popular for meat because the salt helps keep it moist during the cooking process. To the foundation of salt and water, many cooks now add other flavorings to transport taste to every part of the meat (rather than just the exterior, as sometimes happens with a marinade). The same concept holds true for vegetables, fruits, and flowers. Whatever spices you add to fermenting or pickling brine are transported with the salt into the vegetable. This typically results in a unique texture that not everyone likes, so start your brining efforts small until you find a process that's pleasing.

Salt

Table salt and sea salt are most commonly used in brining, and some folks like a gourmet touch like fleur de sel and Hawaiian salt—but these get costly. Recipes will usually specify which salt they recommend. If you're going to substitute, 1 cup of table salt becomes 1½ cups of kosher salt.

Brine Containers

Food-storage containers, large cooking bowls, and stainless-steel stockpots all work very well as brine receptacles. Alternatively, if you're doing a large amount of brining, try a clean cooler (this needs to be sterilized). Remember that you'll need enough brine to completely cover the food. If you can't guess, put the food in the container and cover it with plain water. Measure that water and add your salt accordingly. Note: No matter how much you might like a blend, you should never reuse brine.

Pickle Brining

Pickle brine includes vinegar for curing along with the traditional salt and/ or sugar. Cucumbers are far and away the most popular vegetable for pickling. They are best purchased or harvested unwaxed, when they're small and very firm. Brining waxed cucumbers won't work because the salt cannot penetrate the skin. The basic brine for pickling is 1 quart water to ½ cup salt. It's important that the vegetables remain under the brine throughout the fermenting period. It takes about a month for a whole pickle to be completely fermented. The best test is to cut one open and look for uniform color. See the recipes later in this chapter for specific brining and pickling instructions.

FERMENTATION

Fermentation, or lacto-fermentation, is possibly the most simple, safe, and healthy way to preserve food. It's also one of the oldest methods of food preservation, and almost every culture has a fermented dish in its food repertoire. Kimchi and sauerkraut are probably the two most famous lacto-fermented dishes, and you can ferment any other vegetables, as well as fruit, fish, dairy products, and grains.

Lacto-fermentation differs from other food preservation techniques for two main reasons: the unique taste and the added nutritional benefit that the process creates. Whereas other preservation methods can negatively affect the nutritional value of food, lacto-fermentation results in a finished food product that is packed with essential nutrients, boosts your immune system, and aids digestion by putting healthy bacteria into your body. Lacto-fermentation actually increases significantly the vitamin C levels in some vegetables, such as cabbage.

EQUIPMENT

All you need to start lacto-fermenting food is a cutting board, chopping knife, grater, bowl, noniodized salt, clean water, and either a clean glass jar or ceramic vessel.

PRESERVE.

Dr. Fred Breidt, microbiologist for the USDA Agricultural Research Service, says that lacto-fermented vegetables are actually safer than raw vegetables, which can be exposed to pathogens such as E. coli. Breidt's concern about E. coli applies much less to your backyard veggies than it does to commercial farms, but the point about the safety of lacto-fermentation holds true.

THE FERMENTATION PROCESS

There are essentially three stages to the food lacto-fermentation process. In the first stage, oxygen is removed by anaerobic bacteria (the good bacteria), creating an environment where good bacteria can flourish and bad bacteria cannot survive. In the second stage, lactic acid is produced, effectively killing off any aerobic bacteria (the bad bacteria that will make you sick), as well as creating an environment that allows vitamin C to stabilize. In the third stage, lactic acid increases, the overall pH level decreases further, vitamin C levels increase, and flavor begins to develop, resulting in a mild sauerkraut flavor. To get to this stage takes about a week or less, and at this point the fermented food is ready to eat. If allowed to continue fermenting, and to reach the fourth stage, the pH level will decrease further, and flavor will develop into a bolder taste. It is completely up to you and your taste when you decide to eat your fermented food, but it will be safe and ready to go after just a few days to a week, depending on temperature.

Note: Although you can lacto-ferment many different foods, the following description is specific to vegetables. The same process and steps can be applied to other food groups, although you'll want to do a little research to learn any tricks or recommendations.

Step One: Create Surface Area

Create surface area by chopping, grating, or slicing your veggies, and then place them in a bowl. Sauerkraut is typically grated cabbage, carrots, and chopped garlic, but whether you chop, grate, or slice makes no difference and is entirely up to you.

Step Two: Break Down Cells

The objective here is to help break down cells in the food in order to make it easier for it to be thoroughly penetrated. Depending on what food you are fermenting, you either want to mash it or rub it until it becomes wet. You can mash grated foods between your hands. With some other foods, such as greens, rubbing them in your hands might be more effective. As long as liquid is produced from the food, cells are breaking down and the process is working.

Step Three: Add Salt and Pack It

With your food in the bowl, sprinkle salt on it. It is important that this salt is not iodized, so any sea salt will work. The amount of salt you use depends on your taste, but more salt will slow the fermentation process, and less will speed it up.

Salt will also affect the taste of your food. A good ratio is 1 teaspoon salt per pound of cut vegetables. In most cases, a filled pint jar will equal a pound. If you decide to use whole vegetables, you will want to increase the salt levels, and 1 tablespoon of salt per quart is generally a good ratio.

If you're using cut vegetables, add the salt as you pack it into your glass jar or other vessel. It is very important that you really mash and punch the cut veggies into the vessel so that all air pockets will be removed. After you've filled the container, pour clean water over the food, making sure that all the vegetables are completely covered. With whole vegetables, simply place them into the vessel and pour the saltwater brine over them, making sure to fully submerge the food in liquid. Cover your vessel. If you're using a jar, screw the lid on but be sure to unscrew the top regularly to release the pressure that will build up. This is important! If you're using a ceramic vessel, cover it with a plate but weigh this plate down with something heavy. Otherwise, the pressure will end up moving the plate.

Step Four: Wait

Place your fermentation vessel in a spot where the temperature is between 65°F and 80°F. Most likely this is room temperature, but depending on the season and how warm you keep your house, it can vary. Most likely you will want to wait at least a week before eating your lacto-fermented food, but you can start taste-testing it after day three in order to get a feel for the way the flavor develops. You will also need to check on the food regularly before eating it to remove any mold, to possibly add water, and to release any pressure. If any surface mold develops, simply scrape it off. The food underneath is still totally safe. Add more water if necessary to make sure that your veggies stay submerged, and be sure to release pressure by opening the lids.

Step Five: Eat!

Once your lacto-fermented food reaches the flavor that you like, you can eat it or refrigerate it. Refrigeration will halt the process of fermentation and, therefore, flavor development. Lacto-fermented foods can also be stored in your root cellar, and so long as temperatures don't go above 50°F, it should keep for a very long time wherever you store it.

Keep in mind that lacto-fermentation is an acquired taste for some, and if you don't already love the flavor of sauerkraut, you might want to ease yourself into this preservation technique by allowing foods to ferment for a limited time, so that the flavor is mild. Try lots of different recipes, too. You may find that although you dislike traditional cabbage sauerkraut, you love fermented eggplant or green beans. You might not want all of your preserved food to have the signature lacto-fermented taste, so using this method as one component of your food preservation system works well.

The Recipes

In this section, you'll find recipes for canning, freezing, drying, pickling, and fermenting. Some of these recipes teach you how to preserve your homegrown ingredients and some show you how to use those preserved ingredients in impressively delicious ways. Enjoy!

Blackberry Preserves

This recipe is flexible—use raspberries or a blend of raspberries and blackberries if you prefer.

Yields about 6 pints

3 quarts blackberries

7½ cups granulated sugar

2 3-ounce pouches liquid pectin

1. Rinse fully ripe blackberries in cold water and drain.
2. Place blackberries into a stockpot.
3. Crush with a potato masher to extract juice. Stir in the sugar and mix well.
4. Bring to a full rolling boil over high heat, stirring constantly.
5. Add pectin and return to a full rolling boil. Boil hard for 1 minute.
6. Remove from heat.
7. Skim off foam. Ladle preserves into sterilized jars. Wipe rims. Cap and seal. Process in a water-bath canner for 5 minutes.

Wild Strawberry Preserves

This rustic recipe transports you from your kitchen to the countryside every time you open the lid.

Yields 2½ pints

4 cups ripe strawberries, mashed
4 cups sugar
Optional: 1 tablespoon lemon juice

1. Mix berries and sugar in a bowl and let sit at room temperature for about 1 hour so they begin getting juicy.
2. Transfer to a pan. Add lemon juice and bring to a full rolling boil for 7 minutes, stirring constantly.
3. Pour into 8 presterilized half-pint jars with ¼ inch of headspace. Process in a boiling-water bath for 10 minutes. May be frozen or kept for one year in a dark, cool area.

Green Tomato Raspberry Jam

You can use whatever type gelatin you like in this recipe. No one will ever know there are tomatoes in it!

Yields 8–9 pints

8 cups shredded green tomatoes
½ cup lemon juice
2 teaspoons orange extract
3 tablespoons homemade dried, grated orange peel
8 cups white sugar
2 6-ounce packages raspberry-flavored gelatin mix

1. Combine tomatoes, lemon juice, orange extract, dried orange peel, and sugar in a large saucepan; bring to a boil over medium heat. Stir and cook about 10 minutes.
2. Add gelatin; reduce heat to low and simmer 20 minutes. Spoon into hot, sterilized jars. Cap and seal.
3. Process in a water-bath canner for 10 minutes or pour into freezer containers and freeze.

Corn Relish

Including sweet corn in a zesty relish is a genius way to add color and summer flavor to meals year-round. Serve as a dip for tortilla chips, as a side dish, or spread on a wrap or sandwich.

Yields 5–6 pints

10 cups uncooked sweet baby corn kernels
1 cup sweet red pepper, diced
1 cup sweet green pepper, diced
1 cup celery, diced
½ cup red onion, sliced
½ cup Vidalia onion, diced
1½ cups sugar
2½ cups white vinegar
2 cups water
1 teaspoon salt
2 teaspoons celery seed
2 teaspoons mustard seed

1. Place all ingredients in a large pan over medium heat. Bring to a fast boil; lower heat and simmer 15 minutes.
2. While still hot, pack into pint jars with ½ inch of headspace. Cap and seal.
3. Process in boiling water for 15 minutes. Check lids after cooling for proper sealing.

Spiced Artichoke Hearts

Serve these as appetizers or as a topping to either green salad or pasta salad to add some homegrown charm. The flavor improves if served with a little olive oil.

Yields 4½ pints

2½ cups frozen artichoke hearts, defrosted
¼ cup white wine vinegar
¼ cup red wine vinegar
½ cup water
4 whole cloves garlic
¼ teaspoon thyme
¼ teaspoon parsley
¼ teaspoon rosemary
½ teaspoon basil
½ teaspoon oregano
⅛ teaspoon dried red pepper flakes

1. Blanch the artichoke hearts; chill and drain.
2. Place hearts in equal quantities in 4 half-pint jars.
3. Mix together remaining ingredients; heat in a saucepan to boiling.
4. Pour over hearts, leaving ½ inch of headspace; cap and seal.
5. Process 15 minutes in a hot-water canner. Let cool; then check lids.

Candied Sweet Potatoes

These sweet potatoes taste delicious heated and served with turkey or chicken. The vanilla extract and pumpkin pie spice add just the right kick.

Yields 4 quarts

12 pounds sweet potatoes, scrubbed
Water to cover
5 medium oranges
1½ cups packed brown sugar
1 cup honey
2 tablespoons pure vanilla extract
1½ tablespoons pumpkin pie spice

1. Over medium heat, boil potatoes in water to cover until skins come off easily, about 20 minutes.
2. While potatoes cook, prepare orange sauce. Wash oranges. Grate ¼ cup peel and set aside. Juice oranges and add water to make 2½ cups. In a medium saucepan, combine orange juice mixture, brown sugar, and honey. Bring to a boil over medium-high heat, stirring constantly until sugar dissolves. Stir in vanilla extract, grated orange peel, and pumpkin pie spice. Cover and keep hot.
3. Immerse cooked potatoes in cold water. Rub and pull skins off. Cut potatoes into chunks.
4. Pack potatoes into 1 hot jar at a time, leaving 1 inch of headspace. Ladle ⅓ cup hot syrup into pints and ¾ cup hot syrup into quarts. Remove air bubbles, wipe rims, cap, and seal.
5. Process in a pressure canner at 10 pounds pressure for 65 minutes for pints or 90 minutes for quarts.

Caponata

This is a delightful accompaniment to any meat, fish, or poultry dish. The hint of rosemary really makes this dish pop.

Yields 4 quarts

10 pounds eggplant, peeled and cubed

3½ cups chopped celery

2 cups chopped onion

4 tablespoons extra-virgin olive oil

7 pounds tomatoes, skinned, chopped, and drained

1½ cups red wine vinegar

1 3-ounce can tomato paste

3 tablespoons sugar

2 cups ripe olives, sliced

¾ cup pine nuts or slivered almonds

1 tablespoon minced rosemary

½ cup parsley, finely chopped

3 ounces capers, rinsed and drained

1 teaspoon black pepper

1. Sauté eggplant, celery, and onion in oil until tender.
2. Combine with remaining ingredients in a stockpot. Bring to boil and simmer for 10 minutes.
3. Pack into jars. Remove air bubbles, wipe rims, cap, and seal. Process in a pressure canner at 10 pounds pressure for 30 minutes for pints or 40 minutes for quarts.

Berry Bliss

To improve the flavor of this impressive dish, mix the sugar syrup with berry-flavored juice instead of water. Make sure you use real juice and not juice drinks.

Yields 4 pints

8 cups mixed fresh berries
4 cups Monin sugar syrup

1. Wash berries in cold water; remove any bruised spots.
2. Heat sugar syrup to boiling; fill each jar with ½ cup of liquid. Add berries, leaving ½ inch of headspace and making sure berries are covered in liquid. Remove any air bubbles.
3. Put on lids; process 15 minutes in a hot-water bath.

COOK.

Many fruit recipes call for a sugar syrup. You can make a light syrup by mixing 2 cups of sugar with 1 quart of water (yields 5 cups). A medium syrup is 3 cups of sugar to 1 quart water (5½ cups), and a heavy syrup is 4¾ cups sugar to 1 quart water (6 cups).

Lemon Zesty Pears

Pears and lemon combine to make a topping, side dish, or dessert. The syrup can also be used as part of bastes and marinades if tempered with some vinegar or more lemon juice.

Yields 3 quarts

8 pounds pears
¼ teaspoon Fruit-Fresh (ascorbic acid)
2 cups sugar
⅛ teaspoon grated lemon zest for every 3 pounds pears
4 cups water

1. Wash pears and drain. Peel, core, and halve or quarter. Treat with Fruit-Fresh mixed in water to prevent darkening.
2. To make syrup, in a large stockpot combine sugar, lemon zest, and water; stir well. Heat until boiling; reduce heat to medium. Cook pears until they are tender, 5–6 minutes. Ladle hot pears into sterilized jars, leaving ½ inch of headspace.
3. Ladle hot syrup over pears, leaving ½ inch of headspace. Wipe rims; cap and seal. Process in a water-bath canner 20 minutes for pints or 25 minutes for quarts.

Apple Butter

Fruit butters are a wonderful way to dress up bread, and they can also be used in other ways. In this case, try slathering the butter on ham or a pork chop.

Yields 10 pints

8 pounds apples
4 cups apple cider
4 cups brown sugar
4 cups granulated sugar
4 tablespoons ground cinnamon
1 tablespoon ground cloves
1 tablespoon ground nutmeg
1 teaspoon ground cardamom
½ cup lemon juice

1. Wash apples. Cut off stem and blossom end. Do not peel or core. Cut into small pieces.
2. Add apples and apple cider to a large stockpot. Cover and simmer until apples are soft. Reserve cooking liquid. Press apples through a sieve or a food mill.
3. Return pulp to the stockpot and add the remaining ingredients. Add half the reserved cooking liquid. Cook slowly on medium-low heat 45–60 minutes.
4. As pulp thickens, stir frequently to prevent sticking. If mixture gets too thick, add reserved cooking liquid until you get the desired consistency.
5. Ladle into sterilized jars, leaving ¼ inch of headspace. Wipe rims. Cap and seal. Process in a water-bath canner for 10 minutes.

Blueberry Vinegar

This makes a very unique and beautiful vinegar that has a sweet-sour quality.

Yields 2 quarts

3 cups fresh blueberries
3 cups rice vinegar
2 cinnamon sticks, about 2 inches each
4 whole allspice berries
2 tablespoons honey

1. In a stainless-steel or enamel saucepan, combine 1½ cups blueberries with rice vinegar, cinnamon sticks, and allspice berries. Bring to a boil; reduce heat.
2. Simmer uncovered for 3 minutes. Stir in honey. Remove from heat.
3. Pour mixture through a fine-mesh strainer and let it drain into a bowl. Discard blueberries.
4. Divide remaining 1½ cup blueberries evenly between two jars. Add 1 cinnamon stick and 2 whole allspice berries to each jar.
5. Ladle half of the vinegar into each jar. Remove air bubbles. Wipe rims.
6. Cap and seal in a hot-water bath for 10 minutes. Let sit in a cool place for 2–3 weeks before opening.
7. Strain through a colander lined with cheesecloth twice and discard berries and spices before using.

Candied Ginger

Candied ginger is wonderful in baking, and it also makes a handy breath mint! Note that this basic process also works effectively for fruit, particularly pineapple.

Yields 4 pints

2 pounds fresh gingerroot
1–2 cups cold water to cover
2 cups cold water
1 tablespoon grated lemon zest
4 cups granulated sugar
2 cups superfine sugar

1. Peel gingerroot; cut into very thin strips across the grain. In a saucepan, cover with cold water. Heat to boiling; simmer 5 minutes. Drain.
2. Repeat procedure a second time. Dry on paper towels.
3. In a stockpot, combine 2 cups cold water, lemon zest, and 4 cups granulated sugar. Heat to boiling; simmer 10 minutes, or until a syrup forms.
4. Add ginger; cook slowly until all syrup is absorbed, about 40–50 minutes. Do not boil.
5. Remove ginger; place on a wire rack to dry.
6. Roll ginger in superfine sugar sprinkled on waxed paper; let ginger stand in the sugar until it crystallizes. Spoon into cold, sterilized jars. Cap and seal.

Plum and Walnut Preserves

This is a lovely conserve to enjoy especially in the winter months; the rum-plum blend makes it warm and welcoming.

Yields 9½ pints

4 pounds fresh plums, seeded and quartered
4 fresh limes, very thinly sliced
1½ cups golden raisins
7 cups granulated sugar
2 cups chopped walnuts
8 tablespoons dark rum

1. Add plums, limes, raisins, and sugar to a large stockpot. Cook gently for about 45 minutes or until the mixture is thick. Stir constantly.
2. Remove from heat and stir in chopped walnuts and rum. Let stand about 5 minutes.
3. Ladle into sterilized jars. Cap and seal jars. Process for 10 minutes in a water-bath canner.

Sweet and Sassy Beans

You can make this recipe hotter by using fresh chili peppers. Experiment with various types of beans; each creates a different texture in this recipe.

Yields 8 cups

2 cups white beans
2 cups red beans
2 cups black beans
1½ teaspoons salt
1 cup finely diced onion
1½ cups packed dark brown sugar
1 cup molasses
¼ cup pure maple syrup
2 tablespoons garlic
1 tablespoon Worcestershire sauce
1 tablespoon ginger powder
1 tablespoon spicy brown mustard
1 tablespoon red pepper flakes
Hot sauce to taste
⅓ pound thick bacon, cut in 1-inch pieces

1. Rinse beans. Place in a large pot with 3 quarts water; soak 12 hours.
2. Drain beans. Place back in pan with 3 fresh quarts water and salt. Boil over medium heat; reduce heat and simmer 1 hour.
3. Drain, reserving 2 cups of water for use later.
4. Combine all remaining ingredients; cook slowly, until ingredients are well combined, about 7–10 minutes. Pour over beans along with reserved water.
5. Place in a baking dish; cook at 250°F for 6 hours, stirring periodically. Taste; adjust spices to your liking.
6. Ladle into hot jars with 1 inch of headspace. Remove all air bubbles.
7. Put on tops; process in a pressure cooker at 10 pounds of pressure 1 hour and 20 minutes for pints or 1 hour and 35 minutes for quarts.

Asparagus Appetizer

When you serve this, try it on a bed of baby greens, drizzled with some fresh oil and vinegar and topped with crumbled feta. It's tasty warm or cold.

Yields 1 quart

1½ cups diced white asparagus
1½ cups diced green asparagus
1 tablespoon extra-virgin olive oil
2 teaspoons lemon juice
Zest of ¼ lemon, thinly sliced
¼ teaspoon canning salt
1 bundle scallions, chopped
¼ pound lean ham, cut into tiny bits
Boiling water to cover

1. Rinse, dice, and mix asparagus. Pack into jars with 1 inch of headspace.
2. Mix remaining ingredients together in a pan; gently warm. Spoon into jars evenly; cover everything with boiling water, making sure to leave 1 inch of headspace.
3. Process in a pressure canner 40 minutes at 10 pounds of pressure for quarts.

Blueberry Chutney

This chutney lets you use your blueberries in unexpected ways. Top savory and sweet dishes with this delicious chutney. Try this sweet chutney on goose, turkey, chicken, hen, and other fowl.

Yields 4 pints

8 cups fresh blueberries, rinsed and stemmed
2 medium onions, finely chopped
3 cups red wine vinegar
1 cup golden yellow raisins
1 cup dark brown sugar, firmly packed
1 tablespoon yellow mustard seeds
2 tablespoons freshly grated gingerroot
1 teaspoon ground cinnamon
Pinch of salt
¼ teaspoon ground nutmeg
½ teaspoon dried red pepper flakes

1. Rinse and stem blueberries.
2. Place all ingredients in a large stockpot. Bring mixture to a boil.
3. Lower heat; simmer, stirring occasionally, about 45 minutes, or until chutney is thick.
4. Ladle hot chutney into sterilized jars, leaving ½ inch of headspace. Wipe rims; cap and seal.
5. Process in a water-bath canner for 15 minutes. Cool.
6. Put in a cool, dark place; leave 6–8 weeks before using.

Garlic Jelly

This different kind of jelly can be used as a condiment. It's wonderful added to a marinade or brushed directly on meat while cooking.

Yields 5½ pints

¼ pound peeled garlic cloves
2 cups white vinegar
5 cups granulated sugar
1 3-ounce pouch liquid pectin

1. Blend garlic and ½ cup vinegar in a food processor or blender until smooth.
2. Combine garlic mixture, remaining vinegar, and sugar in a stockpot. Bring mixture to a boil over high heat, stirring constantly.
3. Quickly stir in pectin; return to a boil and boil hard 1 minute, stirring constantly.
4. Remove from heat; ladle into sterilized jars, leaving ¼ inch of headspace. Wipe jar rims; cap and seal.
5. Process in a water-bath canner for 10 minutes.

Caramelized Red Onion Relish

This relish will quickly be a staple condiment in your home. Tangy and sweet, add to any sandwich or use as a spread for bread or crackers.

Yields 6 pints

6 large red onions, peeled and sliced very thinly
¾ cup brown sugar, firmly packed
1 tablespoon extra-virgin olive oil
3 cups dry red wine
½ cup aged balsamic vinegar
½ teaspoon fine sea salt
½ teaspoon freshly ground black pepper

1. In a heavy nonstick skillet, combine onions and sugar with olive oil; heat over medium-high heat.
2. Cook uncovered for 25 minutes, or until onions turn golden and start to caramelize, stirring frequently.
3. Stir in wine, vinegar, salt, and pepper; bring to a boil over high heat. Reduce heat to low; cook 15 minutes, or until most of the liquid has evaporated, stirring frequently.
4. Ladle into sterilized jars, leaving ½ inch of headspace. Remove air bubbles.
5. Wipe rims. Cap and seal. Process in a water-bath canner for 10 minutes.

Vegetable Juice

This healthy beverage can be canned and drunk just like you would commercial vegetable drinks. It can also be frozen.

Yields about 6 quarts

15 pounds fresh, ripe tomatoes, cut up
1 small yellow, orange, or red pepper, chopped
1 small green pepper, chopped
1 cup diced celery
2 diced carrots
2 bay leaves
2 teaspoons dried basil
1 tablespoon salt
1 tablespoon freshly grated horseradish root
½ teaspoon pepper
1 teaspoon sugar
2 teaspoons Worcestershire sauce

1. Put all ingredients in a nonreactive pot (either stainless steel or nonstick); simmer 45 minutes. Stir periodically.
2. Put entire blend through a sieve or juicer to remove any fibers, skins, and seeds. Repeat to get a fine consistency.
3. Return to pan; boil. Pour liquid into hot quart jars, leaving ½ inch of headspace.
4. Process in a hot-water canner for 30 minutes. Let cool; then test lids.

Honey Almond Carrots

This is a delightful side dish for any meal. The orange juice and peel marry well with the sweetness of the carrots.

Yields 3 quarts

8 pounds carrots
6 cups water
3 cups orange juice
¾ cup honey
2 tablespoons pure vanilla extract
½ cup orange peel
⅓ cup sliced almonds
1 tablespoon crystallized ginger

1. Peel and slice carrots. Cook carrots until they are tender but not mushy. Drain and set aside.
2. Prepare syrup by combining water, orange juice, and honey in a saucepan. Bring to a boil and simmer for 10 minutes until syrup starts to thicken slightly. Remove from heat and stir in vanilla. Pack precooked carrots into hot jars.
3. Divide orange peel, sliced almonds, and crystallized ginger evenly among jars. Pour hot syrup over carrots, leaving 1 inch of headspace. Remove air bubbles, wipe rims, cap, and seal.
4. Process in a pressure cooker at 10 pounds pressure for 30 minutes for quarts.

Brandied Plum Jam

The addition of the blackberry brandy really brings out the flavor of the plums in this farm-to-fork dish, but you can use other flavors of brandy if you prefer.

Yields 4 pints

4 pounds plums, pitted and chopped
¾ cup water
2 tablespoons lemon juice
1 package powdered pectin
7 cups sugar
1 cup blackberry brandy

1. Combine plums, water, lemon juice, and pectin in a large stockpot.
2. Bring to a rolling boil over high heat, stirring constantly.
3. Add sugar and return to a rolling boil. Boil hard for 1 minute, stirring constantly.
4. Remove from heat and stir in blackberry brandy.
5. Ladle into sterilized jars, leaving ¼ inch of headspace. Wipe rims. Cap and seal.
6. Process 10 minutes in a water-bath canner.

Raspberry Surprise Preserves

No one will guess that there are beets in this scrumptious preserve. The color is a bright red and the flavor is delightful.

Yields about 7 pints

10 pounds large beets
Cold water to cover beets
7½ cups reserved beet juice
½ cup lemon juice
2 teaspoons grated dried lemon peel
2 packages powdered pectin
5 cups granulated sugar
2 3-ounce packages raspberry Jell-O

1. Cook beets in water until tender. Remove from stockpot with slotted spoon. Reserve juice. When beets are cool, peel, cut into chunks, and purée in a food processor.
2. Measure 7½ cups of reserved beet juice. Add water if necessary.
3. Combine puréed beets, beet juice, lemon juice, grated lemon peel, and pectin. Stir until combined and heat to a boil over medium-high heat.
4. Add sugar and powdered Jell-O. Boil for 8–10 minutes, stirring frequently to prevent scorching. Skim off foam, if necessary.
5. Ladle into sterilized jars, leaving ¼ inch of headspace. Remove air bubbles. Wipe rims. Cap and seal.
6. Process in a water-bath canner for 10 minutes.

Tomato Fritters

These fritters are unique in that they're savory instead of sweet. They freeze nicely in food-storage bags and may be served with any condiment that you enjoy with tomatoes. Try them with a balsamic vinaigrette reduction or a cheese sauce.

Yields 12 fritters

1 cup all-purpose flour
1 teaspoon baking powder
1 teaspoon granulated sugar
Salt to taste
Pepper to taste
¼ teaspoon dried basil
¼ teaspoon dried oregano
1 28-ounce can stewed tomatoes, drained
6 strips turkey bacon, cooked and crumbled
1 tablespoon finely minced onion
½ teaspoon Worcestershire sauce
2 large eggs
Vegetable oil

1. Mix all dry ingredients together. Add tomatoes, bacon, onion, and Worcestershire sauce to the mixing bowl and set aside.
2. Beat the eggs in another bowl. Slowly add them to the tomato-flour mix, stirring as you add them.
3. Fry the fritter batter in hot vegetable oil, 1 tablespoon at a time, in a pan or a deep fryer. Cook until golden brown.
4. Cool and drain on paper towels before freezing.

Herbed Corn on the Cob

Make these at the fall harvest and warm them up on a cold winter day for a lasting taste of summer picnics.

Yields 12 ears

½ cup unsalted butter
1 teaspoon salt and pepper
1 teaspoon parsley
½ teaspoon garlic powder
½ teaspoon onion powder
Optional: ¼ teaspoon chipotle powder
12 ears corn, cleaned and blanched

1. Soften butter; mix in all herbs evenly.
2. Spread the butter evenly over each ear of corn.
3. Wrap cobs tightly with plastic wrap, twisting top and bottom of wrap.
4. Wrap in a layer of aluminum foil. Place in a large resealable food-storage bag in freezer for up to 9 months.
5. When ready to use, take out of food-storage bag and grill or broil in oven safely; the plastic will not melt inside the foil. Defrost first, then warm 15–20 minutes.

Baked Stuffed Potatoes

This recipe comes together quickly and makes a great snack or side dish that's warm and filling. Serve with sour cream, broccoli, or your other favorite potato toppings.

Yields 6 servings

6 large Idaho potatoes, prebaked
¼ cup butter
½ cup green onions, diced
¼ cup crumbled bacon bits
1 cup shredded sharp Cheddar cheese

1. Scoop out insides of potatoes, leaving enough to make a good shell for freezing and baking.
2. Mash potatoes with butter, green onions, bacon bits, and cheese.
3. Refill potato skins, then wrap individually using freezer-safe wrap. Double wrap to avoid freezer burn; label accordingly.
4. To cook, thaw potatoes and warm at 400°F for 30 minutes, until the cheese is fully melted.

Stuffed Sweet Blackened Peppers

These Stuffed Sweet Blackened Peppers are so delicious that your guests won't believe you grew them from seed!

Yields 12 appetizer servings

6 large sweet peppers
1 tablespoon olive oil, plus more for seasoning
Salt, to taste
Ground black pepper, to taste
1 tablespoon butter
½ cup chopped onion
½ cup chopped celery
1 clove garlic, crushed
1 cup tomato sauce
1 teaspoon oregano
½ teaspoon dried leaf basil
1 teaspoon Worcestershire sauce
1½ pounds lean ground beef, cooked and drained
¾ cup shredded cheese

1. Preheat broiler. Place peppers in oven. When skins are bubbly and black, turn over. Remove and cool.
2. Remove blackened exterior of skins. Halve each pepper; season lightly with olive oil, salt to taste, and black pepper to taste. Set aside.
3. In a frying pan, heat 1 tablespoon olive oil and butter; add onions, celery, and crushed garlic. When tender, add tomato sauce, herbs, and Worcestershire; simmer 15 minutes.
4. Add ground beef; remove from heat and cool.
5. Mix in cheese; generously stuff each pepper half with blend.
6. Wrap individually in freezer-safe containers and label. Best used within 4 months.

Minty Nectarine Pear Preserves

Use this for summer pasta salads, poured over pork while it roasts, or as a side dish with various poultry dishes.

Yields 5–6 pints

2 pounds ripe nectarines, peeled and pitted
2 pounds pears, peeled and cored
¾ cup cold water
¼ cup lemon juice
1 teaspoon whole cloves
1 teaspoon whole allspice berries
2 whole cinnamon sticks
5 cups sugar
½ cup fresh mint leaves, chopped, or 2 tablespoons dried mint

1. Peel and pit nectarines; cut into chunks.
2. Peel pears; core. Put in a large stockpot with nectarines, water, and lemon juice.
3. Make a spice ball with cloves, allspice berries, and cinnamon sticks. Add to stockpot; cook over medium heat 10 minutes.
4. Crush nectarines with a potato masher. Add sugar and mint leaves; stir well.
5. Bring mixture to a boil; simmer 15 minutes, until mixture is thick. Remove and discard spice ball.
6. Put into freezer-safe containers with ½ inch of headspace.
7. Alternatively, can this by ladling hot preserves into sterilized jars, leaving ½ inch of headspace. Wipe rims; cap and seal. Process in a water-bath canner for 15 minutes.

Parsley, Sage, Rosemary, and Thyme

This is a great Italian herb blend. Use your own herbs and buy what you don't have at your local farmers' market.

Yields 3½ cups

1 cup fresh parsley
1 cup fresh sage leaves
½ cup fresh rosemary
1 cup fresh thyme

1. Rinse herbs. Blanch for 2–3 seconds. Remove from water when the color of the leaves is noticeably brighter green. Cool and let drip dry.
2. Remove the stalks and mince the parsley, sage, rosemary, and thyme.
3. Freeze in small plastic containers or add herbs to olive oil and freeze in ice cube trays.

Freezer Coleslaw

If you love coleslaw, then keeping a batch from this recipe on hand is an easy way to enjoy this tasty side dish year-round.

Yields 4 pints

1 cabbage
1 carrot
1 green pepper
2 tablespoons pickling salt
1 cup cider vinegar
1¼ cups sugar
¼ cup water
1 teaspoon celery seed

1. Shred the vegetables, sprinkle with salt, and mix well.
2. Cover and let stand for 1 hour. Before the hour is up, mix the vinegar, sugar, water, and celery seed in a saucepan and boil for 1 minute.
3. At the end of the hour, rinse the vegetables with cold water and drain. Squeeze out as much water as you can.
4. In a bowl, pour the brine over the veggie mixture, stir well, and cool.
5. Pack the mixture into containers, leaving 1 inch of headspace, and freeze.

Frozen Strained Tomato Purée

This is the best way to store tomatoes in the freezer, as whole tomatoes will turn to mush after defrosting.

Yield varies

Tomatoes, any amount

1. Wash, core, and quarter your tomatoes.
2. Purée them through a hand-cranked strainer, run them through a food mill, or use a blender; then push them through a sieve to remove seeds and skin.
3. You want a smooth liquid, free of skin and seeds. Pack the liquid into fairly rigid, freezer-safe containers, allowing for 1 inch of headspace. Freeze.

Frozen Stir-Fry Greens

Keeping cooked, frozen greens in the freezer will come in handy when fresh greens aren't available.

Yield varies

Collard greens, any amount
Spinach, any amount

1. Simply wash, sort, and drain your collards and spinach.
2. Cut the greens into strips, removing any thick stems.
3. Stir-fry for 2–3 minutes, just until the greens are wilted.
4. Pack into boilable bags and let them cool. Dry the bags off before putting them in the freezer.

Beet Burgers

These burgers are delicious fresh, but if you're going to make enough for one meal, you might as well stock your freezer. Much more nutritious than any processed veggie burger you can buy at the store, these real vegetable burgers will satisfy even the most devout meat-eater. They are great to have on hand for last-minute meals year-round.

Yields 24 patties

Butter to grease baking sheet

1 cup sesame seeds

4 cups peeled, grated beets

4 cups grated carrots

1 cup minced onion

2 cups sunflower seeds

4 eggs, lightly beaten

2 cups cooked brown rice

2 cups grated Cheddar cheese

1 cup vegetable oil

1 cup fresh parsley, chopped finely

6 tablespoons flour

4 tablespoons tamari

2 garlic cloves

½ teaspoon cayenne pepper

1. Preheat oven to 350°F and lightly grease a baking sheet with butter.
2. Lightly fry the sesame seeds in an ungreased skillet over medium heat—just long enough to release fragrance.
3. Start by mixing the beets, carrots, and onions with your hands in a large bowl. Next, add all the remaining ingredients and continue to mix thoroughly with your hands.
4. Add the cayenne pepper last.
5. Shape your beet mixture into 24 patties and place them on the baking sheet (or as many patties as you can easily fit on the sheet).
6. Bake for about 20 minutes, or until the edges brown. You should not have to turn them unless they are very thick.
7. You can eat some right away, but after cooling, wrap the individual patties in plastic wrap or aluminum foil before putting into a freezer bag or container. Label and put in the freezer.

Frozen Fruit Cups

These Frozen Fruit Cups are healthy summer treats that can also be soothing for little ones with wintertime sore throats.

Yields 20–30 servings

1 watermelon, cut into bite-sized pieces, seeds removed
2 cantaloupes, cut into bite-sized pieces
2 cups berries, washed
½ cup mint leaves, chopped coarsely
3 cups water
4 cups sugar
1 can lemonade concentrate
1 can orange juice concentrate

1. Mix together watermelon, cantaloupe, berries, and mint leaves.
2. Fill individual containers with fruit mixture.
3. Bring water and sugar to a boil, and stir in lemonade and orange concentrates. Pour hot into fruit cups. Cool, seal, and freeze.

Nana's Tomato Sauce

This simple, smooth sauce freezes well. To defrost, simply add the frozen block to a saucepan and heat on low until thoroughly thawed. This sauce is perfect to cook meatballs in—just add baked or pan-fried meatballs to the defrosted sauce and cook on low heat for 1–2 hours. Keep an eye on the pot to make sure the meatballs don't fall apart.

Yields 2 quarts

1 yellow onion, chopped finely
3 or 4 garlic cloves, chopped finely
1 tablespoon olive oil
1 cup tomato purée
1½ cups stewed tomatoes
½ cup tomato paste
Pinch of dried oregano
Pinch of dried basil

1. In a saucepan, sauté the onion and garlic in olive oil until browned.
2. Add the other ingredients and cook on low heat for 20 minutes.
3. Remove from heat and pour into a freezer container. Freeze.

Salsa Verde

More than just a salsa to serve with chips, Salsa Verde is delicious as a chutney or to add flavor and thickness to soups. It also freezes extremely well and is a wonderfully fresh taste to pull from the freezer in wintertime. This boil-only recipe is easily adapted to different batch sizes.

Yields 1 pint

1 pound tomatillos, husked
½ cup finely chopped onion
1 garlic clove, minced
1 serrano chili pepper, minced
2 tablespoons chopped cilantro
1 tablespoon chopped fresh oregano
½ teaspoon ground cumin
1½ teaspoons salt, or to taste
2 cups water

1. Combine all the ingredients and bring to a boil.
2. Reduce heat and simmer for 10–15 minutes.
3. Pour into a blender or food processor and mix until smooth.
4. Pour into freezer containers and transfer to the freezer. To defrost, place in the refrigerator until soft enough to use.

Gazpacho

A classic summer meal, this Gazpacho recipe is rich enough in flavor to serve as a main course, but light and refreshing enough to serve with just about any other dish.

Yields 6–8 servings

4 medium tomatoes, peeled
2 cucumbers, peeled and sliced
½ green bell pepper, seeded and sliced
1 garlic clove, minced
2 tablespoons olive oil
3 tablespoons white wine vinegar
6 slices bread, cubed (whatever bread you prefer)
3½ cups water
4 ice cubes
1½ teaspoons pepper

1. Mix all ingredients in a blender or food processor until smooth. Don't worry if it is a little too thick; you can add water when you defrost it.
2. Pour into freezer-safe containers and store. To defrost, put in the refrigerator and serve chilled.

Eggplant Casserole

The ultimate comfort food on a cold winter day is a warm, filling casserole. One that only needs to be moved from the freezer to the oven is even better.

Yields 10–12 servings

1 large eggplant
3 eggs, beaten
1 cup dry bread crumbs
Olive oil
¾ cup Parmesan cheese
½ pound mozzarella cheese, sliced
2 teaspoons dried oregano, or 1 tablespoon fresh
3 cups tomato sauce

1. Preheat oven to 350°F.
2. Peel the eggplant and slice into ¼-inch slices, and place in a bowl.
3. Pour the beaten eggs over the eggplant pieces, making sure to coat evenly.
4. Coat the eggplant in bread crumbs. Heat the oil in a skillet until hot. Pan-fry the eggplant until golden brown. Remove from heat.
5. Layer the eggplant in a casserole dish with the Parmesan, mozzarella, and oregano.
6. Cover with tomato sauce. Bake for 20 minutes. Let cool to room temperature. Wrap the casserole dish in aluminum foil, followed by layers of plastic wrap. Label and freeze. To reheat, bake at 350°F until hot all the way through.

Tomato Corn Casserole

This homegrown recipe is easy to make when there is excess harvest during the summer.

Yields 8 servings

2½ cups tomatoes, peeled
2½ cups loose corn kernels, cooked
1 green bell pepper, chopped
½ cup dry bread crumbs
2 tablespoons melted butter
1 teaspoon onion salt
Pinch of black pepper
½ cup Cheddar cheese, grated

1. Combine the tomatoes, corn, bell pepper, bread crumbs, and melted butter.
2. Stir in onion salt and black pepper.
3. Add to a greased casserole dish and top with cheese. Wrap and freeze. To bake, place frozen casserole in the oven and bake at 350°F until browned and heated all the way through.

Millet and Butternut Squash Casserole

Slightly sweet, slightly savory, this casserole is great to pull out of the freezer for a cool-weather dinner.

Yields 4 servings

1 cup millet
2 cups vegetable broth
1 small butternut squash, peeled, seeded, and chopped
½ cup water
1 teaspoon curry powder
½ cup orange juice
½ teaspoon sea salt

1. In a small pot, cook millet in vegetable broth until done, about 20–30 minutes.
2. In a separate pan, heat butternut squash in water. Cover and cook for 10–15 minutes until squash is almost soft. Remove lid and drain extra water.
3. Combine millet with squash over low heat and add curry and orange juice, stirring to combine well. Heat for 3–4 more minutes and season with sea salt.
4. Allow to cool to room temperature, and pour into a freezer-safe baking dish. Wrap well, label, and freeze. To defrost, unwrap the dish, leaving aluminum foil in place, and bake at 350°F for 45 minutes or until done.

Bell Peppers Stuffed with Couscous

Baked, stuffed peppers grown in your garden are delicious and filling, and make for a great individually packaged frozen meal.

Yields 4 servings

4 cups water or vegetable broth
3 cups couscous
2 tablespoons olive oil
2 tablespoons lemon or lime juice
1 cup frozen peas or corn, thawed
2 green onions, sliced
½ teaspoon cumin
½ teaspoon chili powder
4 green bell peppers

1. Bring water or vegetable broth to a boil and add couscous. Cover, turn off heat, and let sit for 10–15 minutes until couscous is cooked. Fluff with a fork.
2. Combine couscous with olive oil, lemon or lime juice, peas or corn, green onions, cumin, and chili powder.
3. Cut tops off bell peppers and remove seeds.
4. Stuff couscous into bell peppers and place the tops back on, using a toothpick to secure if needed.
5. Freezer-wrap each pepper in a layer of foil, followed by plastic wrap. Store in freezer bags and put in the freezer.
6. To defrost, preheat oven to 350°F and transfer pepper(s) to a baking dish; remove plastic wrap, leaving one layer of aluminum foil on. Bake for 15 minutes, remove foil, and continue baking until brown.

Perfect Peaches and Pears

Some recipes for freezer jelly use cornstarch as a thickener. Cornstarch, however, lends the jelly a completely different texture, so this recipe relies on pectin.

Yields 10 cups

3 ripe pears, not mushy

3 small ripe peaches

1 teaspoon orange juice

1 teaspoon orange peel

1 teaspoon lemon peel

1 tablespoon freshly grated gingerroot

2 cups sugar

2 cups water

1 pouch dry pectin

1. Peel the pears and peaches and dice them.
2. Combine pears, peaches, juice, orange and lemon peels, and ginger in a saucepan. Cook over medium-low heat until the fruit is fully tender.
3. Add sugar and water and bring to a boil for 15 minutes. Add pectin and boil for 1 minute more.
4. Remove from heat and cool slightly before transferring to freezer containers. Leave ½ inch of headspace. Use within 3 months.

Plumberry Jam

This Plumberry Jam is guaranteed to be a farm-to-fork favorite at your table. And feel free to use whatever fruits you have in season. For example, you can substitute 1 cup of blueberries for the strawberries, if desired.

Yields 4 pints

2 cups red raspberries
1 cup strawberries
1 cup peeled, diced ripe plum
5 cups sugar
½ cup light corn syrup
¾ cup water
1 3-ounce package powdered fruit pectin

1. Mix the fruit together with the sugar and let stand for 15 minutes.
2. Place the fruit in a pan with corn syrup and water. Bring to a boil.
3. Add pectin and continue boiling for 1 minute. Cool and put into containers. Leave ½ inch of headspace and freeze.

Dried Hot Pepper Flakes

This is a good way to use up those leftovers from the garden. It doesn't matter how many varieties you mix together.

Yields 1 cup

5 cups fresh hot peppers, any variety

1. Rinse any lingering dirt off peppers.
2. Remove pepper stems and ends; clean off seeds.
3. Chop peppers no more than ¼ inch thick.
4. Line a cookie sheet with heavy-duty aluminum foil; lightly spray with cooking spray. Evenly spread chopped peppers onto cookie sheet.
5. Place in a 200°F oven. Leave oven door slightly ajar. Bake 3–4 hours, turning with a long-handled spatula every 30 minutes. Peppers should be bone dry.
6. Leave on kitchen counter for a few days to make sure flakes crumble when picked up. Store in a Mason jar with a tight-fitting cover. Label clearly.

PRESERVE.

Hot peppers can be dangerous if you do not handle them properly. Always wear disposable rubber gloves when you handle them, and never touch your eyes or mouth. Hot peppers leave behind an oily residue that can cause a burning sensation if it comes into contact with your skin, eyes, or mouth.

Vegetable Chips

This recipe makes a healthy snack that has a long shelf life and can also double as the base for a vegetable soup or stew.

Yields about 10 cups

2 large potatoes, thinly sliced
1 sweet potato, peeled and thinly sliced
3 large radishes, peeled and thinly sliced
2 thick carrots, peeled and thinly sliced
2 thick parsnips, peeled and thinly sliced
2 tablespoons olive oil
½ teaspoon salt
1 teaspoon garlic powder

1. Blanch vegetables for 1 minute; drain.
2. Toss slices with olive oil, salt, garlic powder, and any other spices you like.
3. Sort in layers by vegetable type and transfer to a dehydrator, using the temperature setting recommended by the manufacturer. Dry about 6 hours, until crispy.
4. Store in an airtight container.

Citrus Peels

This rustic dish is a great way to use peels. In dried form, these are excellent in canning and preserving recipes, as well as for baking.

Yield varies

Citrus peels (orange, lemon, lime, tangerine, grapefruit)

1. Shred peels; leave in a cool, dry room to dry, covered with a paper plate.
2. Use a food processor or grinder to chop peels into a good size for cooking. Put in an airtight container; label and store.

Culinary Herbs

It's best to dry your herbs separately and make them into blends afterward because some dry at different rates than others. This basic method works for drying fresh mushrooms, too.

Yields 1 teaspoon

1 tablespoon fresh-picked herbs

1. Pick herbs early in the day. Strip off stems; chop finely. Reserve stems to use in aromatic potpourri or discard.
2. Place on a cookie sheet with aluminum foil sprayed lightly with cooking spray. Put into a 200°F oven with door slightly ajar. Turn over with a long-handled pancake turner every 15–20 minutes for 2 hours.
3. Leave the dry herbs covered on the counter 2–3 days to make sure they're completely bone-dry.
4. Transfer into labeled jars or blend and put into jars.

Fruit Leather

This is a great way to use up berries that are in less-than-perfect condition. You can use combinations of different fruits or even vegetables.

Yield varies based on ingredients used

Fruit, any kind
Honey, to taste
Water, as needed

1. Simply make a purée of fruit and sweetener (sugar or honey work well, and you can use as much or as little as you like) that is thin enough to pour (add water or juice if necessary).
2. Place parchment paper on your dehydrator sheets and pour the purée out, spreading it across the tray. You will want to make the edges twice as thick as the center as the edges will dry out first.
3. Turn your dehydrator to a low heat, about 135°F, depending on the specific berry or fruit combination, and let it run until you can easily remove the fruit from the paper in one piece and it is not sticky to the touch (usually 4–6 hours).
4. When rolled and wrapped up in plastic wrap or wax paper, your fruit leather can last for 6–8 weeks in the refrigerator.

Candied Strawberries

You can use any berries you like for this recipe, but if you're making a combination, be sure to separate the berries inside the dehydrator in case one type is ready first.

Yields ½ cup

1 pint fresh strawberries
¼ pound sugar

1. Slice the strawberries and dip each berry into the sugar.
2. Dry according to your dehydrator instructions, usually around 130°F for at least 6 hours.

Tomato Basil Flax Crackers

These crackers are great to serve with cheese or spreads as an appetizer or as a nutrient-rich snack on a camping or hiking trip.

Yields 8 servings as a snack

8 dried tomatoes, cut into pieces and soaked for 30 minutes
⅓ red bell pepper
1 tablespoon olive oil
1 teaspoon sea salt
2 fresh tomatoes, chopped
1 red onion, chopped
1 garlic clove, pressed
¼ cup basil
Salt and pepper to taste
Cayenne to taste
1 cup golden flaxseed, soaked for at least 2 hours

1. Using a food processor, mix all ingredients except for the flaxseed.
2. Once everything is well mixed, add the seed by hand. Spread the mixture onto your dehydrator sheets, evenly but not too thinly.
3. Dry at 110°F for 8–12 hours.
4. Turn over and continue drying for another 8 hours.

Sweet Potato Bark

This Sweet Potato Bark is a great recipe for a snack, to add to a meal, or to take on a backpacking trip.

Yields ¾ cup

1 large sweet potato, peeled and cut into chunks
½ cup apple juice
3 tablespoons maple syrup
½ teaspoon cinnamon
½ teaspoon nutmeg

1. Boil the sweet potato chunks until soft enough to mash.
2. Stir in the other ingredients and use either a mixer or blender to mix until completely smooth.
3. Spread the purée to ⅛-inch thickness on dehydrator sheets and dry at 135°F for at least 8 hours.
4. Turn over halfway through, at about 5 hours.

Dried Tomatoes and Herb Quiche

Use your own dried tomatoes and herbs in this delicious recipe. The result is an amazing quiche that you'll want to share with your friends and family.

Yields 6–8 servings

1 unbaked pastry shell
¾ cup dried tomatoes (home-dried, not in oil)
Boiling water
1 tablespoon olive oil
½ cup finely chopped onion
1½ cups chopped spinach
1 garlic clove, minced
1 teaspoon dried basil
½ teaspoon dried thyme
1½ cups grated Gruyère cheese
5 large eggs, at room temperature
1½ cups light cream
½ teaspoon salt
¼ teaspoon pepper

1. Preheat oven to 425°F.
2. Put pastry shell into a 9-inch pie pan. Bake for 10 minutes. Once you take the crust out of the oven, lower the heat to 325°F.
3. While the oven cools, cut dried tomatoes into small pieces using scissors.
4. To rehydrate, pour boiling water over the tomatoes, cover, and let sit for 10 minutes before draining the water.
5. Heat olive oil over medium heat in a skillet.
6. Add the onion and cook for 3 minutes, then add the tomatoes, spinach, garlic, basil, and thyme. Cook just until the spinach wilts.
7. Fill the pastry shell with this mixture and cover with cheese. In a large bowl, whisk the eggs, cream, salt, and pepper. Pour over the cheese. Bake for 40 minutes until golden brown.

Cheesy Dried Potato Chips

Cheesy and filling, these chips are so delicious you won't be able to stop snacking on them!

Yields approximately 2 cups

3 cups potatoes, peeled, boiled, and mashed
1½ cups sharp Cheddar cheese, grated
½ cup Parmesan cheese, grated
½ teaspoon salt

1. Combine all ingredients in a food processor and mix until smooth.
2. Spread onto dehydrator sheets and dry at 145°F for at least 5 hours.
3. Turn sheet over in the fourth hour, or when one side is dry.

Dried Sour Cream and Onion Chips

Slightly chewier than traditional sour cream and onion chips, these chips are a zesty, tangy, and satisfying snack.

Yields 2–3 cups

4 cups potatoes, peeled, boiled, and mashed
1 cup plain yogurt
¼ cup onion, chopped
½ teaspoon salt

1. Combine all ingredients in a food processor and mix until smooth.
2. Spread onto dehydrator sheets and dry at 145°F for at least 5 hours.
3. Turn sheet over in the fourth hour, or when one side is dry.

Salad Topping

You do not have to be exactly precise with this farm-to-table recipe. Just use up your vegetable ends and pieces and toss them with a little seasoning.

Yields about 4 cups

1½ cups sweet peppers, diced
1 cup green onions, diced
1 cup red onions, diced
1 cup celery, chopped
1 cup carrots, chopped
1 cup cherry tomatoes, quartered
1 cup cabbage, diced
Optional: ½ cup banana pepper, diced
1 teaspoon Worcestershire sauce
Optional: 1 teaspoon garlic powder
1 teaspoon salt
1 teaspoon ground pepper
2 tablespoons sesame seeds
2 tablespoons sunflower seeds
½ cup chow mein noodles

1. Preheat oven to 150°F. If you are using a dehydrator, follow the manufacturer's suggested setting for vegetables.
2. In a bowl, mix all ingredients except the sesame seeds, sunflower seeds, and noodles; toss vegetables to evenly coat in the spices.
3. Spread mixture evenly onto nonstick cooking trays. Dry in the oven; stir periodically to make sure nothing sticks or burns.
4. When the mixture is crunchy (about 3–4 hours), cool and mix with sesame seeds, sunflower seeds, and noodles.
5. Store in an airtight container with the rest of your spices. The topping has a shelf life of 6 months.

Brown Sauce Sheets

These roll-up-style sauce sheets can be sliced and placed over meat while it's cooking or used a little at a time in soups and stews for additional flavor.

Yields 5 cups

1 tablespoon olive oil

2 large sweet onions, roughly chopped

Optional: Sugar to taste

½ cup tamarind paste

2 tablespoons garlic, minced

2 tablespoons ginger, minced

¼ cup tomato paste

2 tablespoons freshly cracked black pepper

½ cup dark corn syrup

1 cup blackstrap molasses

2 cups white vinegar

1 cup balsamic vinegar

1 cup dark beer

½ cup orange juice

¼ cup soy sauce

2 tablespoons coarsely ground mustard

2 tablespoons liquid smoke

2 cups low-fat beef stock

1. Heat olive oil in a frying pan. Add onions; sauté until soft. If you like a sweeter sauce, sprinkle a few pinches of sugar on them as they sauté.
2. Put onions and all remaining ingredients in a large saucepan; bring to a boil. Stir regularly.
3. Reduce to a simmer. Continue to stir regularly over the next 2–3 hours until it reduces by about 1 cup. Increase simmering time for a thicker sauce with more concentrated flavors.
4. Place an even coating of the sauce on waxed paper or the fruit roll-up sheets of your dehydrator. For the latter, follow the manufacturer's recommended temperature. If drying in the oven, set the temperature for 150°F; cook until no longer sticky. This can take up to 12 hours depending on the environment.
5. Slice to preferred sizes. Wrap in waxed paper; store in a jar or food-storage bag for future use.

Traditional Dilly Beans

These are often a seasonal favorite. For a change of tastes, try using these pickles as the base for a green bean casserole.

Yields 4 pints

2 pounds fresh green beans, trimmed
8 dill weed sprigs
4 cloves garlic
4 teaspoons pickling salt
2 cups white vinegar
½ cup red wine vinegar
2½ cups water

1. Cut beans to fit the jars. Blanch beans for 3 minutes, then move to an ice bath. Drain. Pack beans into sterilized jars. Place two sprigs of dill and one clove of garlic in each jar.
2. In a saucepan, mix the salt, vinegars, and water; bring to a boil. Pour over the beans, leaving ½ inch of headspace.
3. Fit the lids and process for 10 minutes in a hot-water bath.

Sweet Minted Eggplant

These pickles do not need to be chilled for serving. In fact, they're tastiest at room temperature.

Yields about 3 cups

1 pound small eggplants, cut into ½-inch-thick rounds
1 tablespoon pickling salt
2 tablespoons lemon juice
2 tablespoons distilled white vinegar
2 tablespoons honey
½ cup extra-virgin olive oil
2 tablespoons minced garlic
⅓ cup chopped fresh mint
Grated zest of 1 lemon
¼ teaspoon dried red pepper flakes
Salt to taste
Black pepper to taste

1. Sprinkle eggplant slices with pickling salt; let stand 30 minutes.
2. Preheat oven broiler.
3. Mix lemon juice, vinegar, honey, olive oil, herbs, and salt and pepper, to taste, together; toss eggplant pieces to coat evenly.
4. Remove eggplant; grill lightly 3 minutes on each side.
5. Toss back into honey-vinegar blend; pack into a small jar. Pickles can be refrigerated for several months.

COOK.

Eggplant is a member of the nightshade family, so it is related to tomatoes and potatoes. When you shop for eggplants, look for fruits with smooth, firm skin. The skin should give when you press it gently, but it should not be mushy or discolored.

Green Tomato Piccalilli

This can be served as a side dish or as a brightly colored condiment, especially for hamburgers and hot dogs.

Yields 6–8 pints

16 cups green tomatoes, finely chopped
½ head green cabbage, finely chopped
½ cup pickling salt
Water to cover vegetables
4 cups cider vinegar
1½ cups dark brown sugar
½ tablespoon yellow mustard seed
½ tablespoon ground cinnamon
1 tablespoon black pepper
⅛ teaspoon crushed red pepper flakes
½ tablespoon ground allspice
1 tablespoon ground ginger
1 tablespoon dill seed

1. Combine vegetables and salt; cover with water and soak overnight. Drain and rinse vegetables.
2. In a large pot, combine remaining ingredients; bring to a boil. Add drained vegetables; return mixture to a boil. Reduce heat; simmer until vegetables are tender, about 30 minutes.
3. Pack hot mixture into sterilized pint jars. Cover; process in boiling bath for 15 minutes.

PRESERVE.

Traditional piccalilli is a mixture of chopped vegetables with piquant spices such as mustard. Common components include cabbage, tomato, cauliflower, carrot, and onion, but nearly anything can go into the pickling mixture.

Gracious Garlic Dills

Nothing goes together quite so well as homegrown dill and garlic. These Gracious Garlic Dills are perfect on your favorite sandwich, but are also amazing right out of the jar.

Yields 8 quarts

8 pounds pickling cucumbers
12 cups ice water
4 cups white vinegar
⅔ cup pickling salt
16 whole cloves garlic
4 teaspoons minced garlic
16 sprigs fresh dill weed
4 teaspoons dry dill weed

1. Wash cucumbers and soak in ice water for 2 hours. If you're planning to slice cukes, wait until just before canning.
2. Bring the vinegar, water, and salt to a boil.
3. Place 2 cloves of garlic, ¼ teaspoon minced garlic, 2 sprigs of fresh dill, and ¼ teaspoon dry dill into each of the 8 quart jars. Pack each jar with approximately 1 pound of cucumbers.
4. Fill jars with brine, leaving 1 inch of headspace and making sure the cucumbers are fully covered.
5. Cap and process jars for 15 minutes in a hot-water bath. Age for 2 months before eating.

Dad's Freezer Pickles

This recipe is highly adaptable; you can tinker with other spices and add other seasonable vegetables to the blend.

Yields 2 quarts

12 cups thinly sliced cucumbers
4 cups thinly sliced sweet onions
3 cups sugar
3 cups vinegar
1 teaspoon canning salt
1 teaspoon mustard seed
1 teaspoon celery seed

1. Place cucumbers and onions in a large nonreactive bowl.
2. Mix remaining ingredients in a saucepan; bring to a boil. Stir to dissolve sugar.
3. Pour over cucumbers. Put a plate on top of cucumbers so they stay below brine; let sit at room temperature 24 hours.
4. Move into freezer-safe containers. This blend can be successfully canned using a hot-water-bath method for 15 minutes.

Watermelon Pickles

This is a Southern favorite that has a fresh, thirst-quenching quality. After all, nothing tastes better than a watermelon that you've grown yourself.

Yields 5 pints

4 pounds watermelon rind
½ cup pickling salt
8 cups water
4 cups sugar
2 cups white vinegar
5 ½-inch cinnamon sticks
10 whole cloves
5 ¼-inch slices gingerroot, peeled
1 lemon, sliced into 5 pieces

1. Trim the pink parts off the watermelon rind; cube rind.
2. Soak the rind in pickling salt and water overnight; drain and rinse thoroughly.
3. Place rind in a large pot and cover with water; simmer until tender, being careful not to overcook.
4. In a large stockpot, mix remaining ingredients; simmer 10 minutes.
5. Add watermelon rind, cooking over low heat until nearly transparent.
6. Transfer rind and liquid to half-pint jars. Leave ½ inch of headspace; process in a hot-water bath for 10 minutes.

Pickled Peaches and Pears

This farm-to-fork recipe is so unique, your guests will be asking for Mason jars of it to take home!

Yields 4 quarts

4 cinnamon sticks
8 whole cloves
4 ¼-inch slices fresh ginger
5 cups sugar
2½ cups vinegar
2½ cups water
8 cups peaches, peeled and pitted
8 cups pears, peeled and pitted

1. Prepare your sterilized quart jars beforehand by putting 1 whole stick of cinnamon, 2 whole cloves, and 1 slice of gingerroot in each.
2. Combine sugar, vinegar, and water; bring to a boil.
3. After 10 minutes add fruit; cook until partially tender.
4. Pack fruit into jars, pouring syrup over top and leaving ½ inch of headspace.
5. Add tops; process 10 minutes in a hot-water bath.

Pickled Garlic and Onions

This recipe makes a nice snack, or it may be used in garnishing various beverages, such as a delicious dry martini.

Yields 2½ pints

12 large garlic cloves
12 pearl onions
2 cups white vinegar
½ cup red wine vinegar
1 cup dry white wine
1 tablespoon pickling salt
1 tablespoon sugar
Optional: 1 tablespoon oregano or basil

1. Blanch garlic and onions 30 seconds. Immediately transfer to ice bath; drain and peel.
2. Bring vinegars, wine, salt, sugar, and spices to a boil for 1 minute.
3. Separate garlic and onions evenly between prepared canning jars.
4. Pour hot brine over onions and garlic, leaving ½ inch of headspace. Cap.
5. Process in a hot-water bath for 10 minutes. Cool; label and store.

Pickled Beets

Pickled beets are intense in flavor and texture. The perfect blend of softness and firmness, pickled beets are a great addition to sandwiches and salads, as well as being a delicious side for meat dishes.

Yields 8 quarts

6–10 medium-sized beets or enough to fill 8 quart-sized jars

4 cups beet juice (can be diluted with water if necessary)

2 cups vinegar

4 cups sugar

1 teaspoon salt

1. Boil the beets until you can easily insert a fork into them, about 20 minutes.
2. Mix the beet juice, vinegar, sugar, and salt and boil this liquid mixture.
3. Add the beets to the liquid and continue cooking until beets are soft enough to eat, about 10 minutes.
4. Pack the beets into the jars and cover with beet juice mixture, being sure to leave ½–1 inch of headspace.
5. Submerge the jars in boiling water long enough to seal the lids.

Fermented Mint Chutney

Whether you're hunting, raising your own livestock, or shopping at your local farmers' market, this chutney is wonderful as a topping to any meat dish.

Yields 3 cups

2 cups fresh mint leaves
1 onion, coarsely chopped
4 garlic cloves, coarsely chopped
4 jalapeño chilies, seeded and chopped
⅔ cup almonds, finely chopped
1 tablespoon sea salt
1 cup water

1. Use a food processor to mix all the ingredients except salt and water.
2. Place in a glass quart jar and press down lightly to remove any air bubbles.
3. Mix salt and water and pour into the jar, covering the chutney. Allow 1 inch of headspace and cover tightly. To allow flavor to develop, wait at least 2 days before putting in the refrigerator.

Pickled Garlic Scapes

Use only the most tender garlic scapes from your garden to enjoy in this simply delicious recipe.

Yields 1 quart

About 1½ teaspoons unrefined sea salt
1 quart water
Enough tender garlic scapes, trimmed with hard stems removed, to fit in a 1-quart jar

1. Stir sea salt together with 1 quart fresh water until the salt is dissolved.
2. Pack a glass quart jar with the garlic scapes.
3. Pour the saltwater over the scapes, completely covering them. Ferment for a minimum of a week, and up to 4 weeks, to achieve the flavor you like.

Fiery Fermented Jalapeños

These Fiery Fermented Jalapeños are not for the faint of heart! However, they are delicious so be sure to find a place for them at your table.

Yields 1 quart

1 quart fresh jalapeño peppers
½ onion, sliced
3 or 4 cloves garlic
3 tablespoons sea salt
1 quart water

1. Gently wash and clean the jalapeños, sorting out any bruised or damaged peppers.
2. Pack the peppers, onion, and garlic into a quart jar or ceramic crock.
3. Combine the salt and water until the salt is dissolved. Pour this brine over the vegetables, making sure they are fully submerged.
4. Cover your container and store at room temperature. Wait for the peppers to turn an olive green, in about 5–7 days, before tasting.

Fermented Salsa

This tangier, fermented version of classic, fresh salsa is a must-serve at your next farm-to-table dinner—or any day of the week!

Yields 1 quart

4 large tomatoes, peeled, seeded, and diced
2 onions, finely chopped
¾ cup chili pepper, chopped
8 garlic cloves, finely chopped
1 bunch cilantro, chopped
Juice of 2 lemons
2 tablespoons sea salt
¼ cup water

1. Pack all ingredients except salt and water into a quart-sized jar. Pack well, and if necessary, use a meat hammer to ensure that all air bubbles are out.
2. Mix salt and water and pour over the vegetables, making sure to fully submerge. Allow 1 inch of space between the veggies and the top of the jar. Cover and check the taste after the second day.

Kimchi (Korean Sauerkraut)

Kimchi is an important Korean dish, served at every meal. Thin-leafed napa cabbage is the traditional cabbage used in kimchi, and it can easily be grown in many North American climates.

Yields 2 quarts

1 head napa cabbage, cored and shredded
1 bunch green onions, chopped
1 cup carrots, grated
1 tablespoon freshly grated ginger
3 garlic cloves, minced
½ teaspoon dried chili flakes
2 tablespoons sea salt

1. Combine everything in a large bowl.
2. Using your hands or a meat hammer, pound the mixture to release juices. Continue pounding until the juices are just below the top of the mixture.
3. Pack into quart-sized jars and pour water over, fully submerging the vegetable mixture. Allow 1 inch of headspace before covering with lids. Keep at room temperature for at least 3 days before refrigerating.

Sauerkraut

This rustic sauerkraut recipe pairs perfectly with sausages and hot dogs, or works well as a hearty side dish to any meal.

Yields 1 quart

1 medium cabbage, cored and shredded
1 tablespoon caraway seeds
2 garlic cloves
2 tablespoons sea salt

1. Mix all the ingredients in a bowl using your hands and a meat pounder. Pound and squeeze the mixture until the juices begin to fill the bowl.
2. Pack tightly into a quart jar and pour water in until the mixture is submerged. Allow 1 inch of space between the top of the cabbage mixture and the top of the jar. Ferment for at least 3 days before refrigerating.

Pickled Ginger

You can enjoy pickled ginger on its own, not only with sushi. Pair it with meat and fish dishes at home.

Yields 1 quart

3 pounds fresh gingerroot
2 tablespoons sea salt
1 quart water

1. Using a vegetable peeler, peel the ginger and slice it very thinly.
2. Place the slices in a bowl and using a meat pounder, pound the ginger to release juices.
3. Pack into a quart jar, pressing down as you pack.
4. Mix the salt with the water and pour over the ginger. Allow 1 inch of room at the top of the jar and cover. Wait at least 3 days before refrigerating.

Sour Berry Syrup

This fermented version of classic berry syrup has a tangy sweet-and-sour taste that is delicious on ice cream, pastries, or pancakes.

Yields 1 quart

4 cups fresh berries (anything other than strawberries, which are too acidic)
3 teaspoons sea salt
¼ cup sugar
2 teaspoons pectin

1. Wash berries and place in a bowl with the other ingredients.
2. Mash until well crushed.
3. Pour the mixture into a quart jar and push down lightly. Pour in enough water to just reach the same level as the berries. Make sure the tops of the berries are 1 inch from the top of the jar, and cover. After 2 days at room temperature, taste and transfer to the refrigerator.

Snap Beans

Use only fresh, tender green beans in this recipe. The ones you grow yourself will taste best!

Yields 1 quart

Enough green beans to fill a quart jar, trimmed
2 small dried hot peppers
2 garlic cloves, chopped
4 whole black peppercorns, crushed
2 dill heads
2 tablespoons sea salt
Water

1. Pack all the ingredients into a quart jar.
2. Cover with water, making sure to submerge all the vegetables. Allow 1 inch of room between the tops of the beans and the top of the jar. Cover and keep at room temperature for at least 3 days before tasting.

Sour Mustard Greens

This Vietnamese dish is mild, with a lighter fermented taste than most lacto-fermented foods.

Yields 2 quarts

1½ pounds mustard greens, cut into small pieces
6 scallions, cut into small pieces
1 quart water
1 tablespoon sea salt

1. Wilt the greens and scallions slowly at a low heat in the oven, or if it's a warm day you can put them outside in the sun.
2. Mix the water and salt until the salt is dissolved. Once the greens are wilted, pack in quart jars, layering the greens with the brine.
3. Make sure the greens are completely submerged and allow 1 inch of space at the top.
4. Cover the jar and store at room temperature for 3–4 days or until the greens are sour enough. Refrigerate.

Pickled Cherry Tomatoes

This Russian tomato recipe works best with tomatoes that are not yet fully ripe.

Yields 2 quarts

1¾ pounds cherry tomatoes
5 or 6 dill heads
¼ cup horseradish, coarsely grated
5 garlic cloves, halved
3 sprigs parsley
3 sprigs tarragon
½ fresh hot pepper, seeded
Several dill sprigs
2 tablespoons sea salt
1 quart water

1. Pack all the ingredients into quart jars, except for the salt and water.
2. Mix the salt in the water until dissolved, then pour over the tomato mixture. Use just enough brine to fully cover the tomatoes.
3. Allow at least 1 inch of space between the top of the tomatoes and the top of the jar.
4. Let the jars sit at room temperature for at least a week before tasting. Refrigerate.

APPENDIX A

PRODUCE PRESERVATION INFORMATION

As you know, different types of produce do best when preserved in different ways. The following information will serve as a preserving reference as you prepare your garden's bounty for future use.

VEGETABLES

- **Artichokes:** Artichokes are best eaten fresh or pickled.
- **Asparagus:** Asparagus can be dried or pickled.
- **Beans:** Fresh beans won't last for much more than a week in your refrigerator, but they can be stored easily either by drying (preferred) or by canning or freezing.
- **Beets:** To store beets you can pickle them, can them, or keep them in a root cellar.
- **Broccoli:** The best way to store broccoli is by freezing. Before going into the freezer, broccoli should be soaked in saltwater to remove dirt and pests. After soaking for about 30 minutes, the broccoli can be chopped into smaller pieces.
- **Brussels Sprouts:** To store Brussels sprouts indoors, you want to leave the roots attached to the plants and hang them upside down in your root cellar as soon as they are harvested.
- **Cabbage:** Cabbage is great pickled, frozen, or canned.
- **Carrots:** When storing carrots, you need to remove the green, leafy tops. This is true whether you are storing them in your fridge (where they will keep in a sealed plastic bag for several weeks or more), freezing them (blanch them first), canning them (you will need to use a pressure cooker), or storing in your root cellar (carrots buried in sand and stored in a root cellar will keep for several months).
- **Collards:** Collards can be dried, frozen, or canned.
- **Corn:** Corn tastes best when eaten fresh, but is still worth preserving. You can easily freeze the kernels for several months. You can also dry corn on the cob and use the individual cobs for popcorn for up to a year.
- **Cucumbers:** Cucumbers can only be preserved in a brine and then either frozen or canned.
- **Eggplants:** Eggplants are best frozen or dried.
- **Kale:** Kale is best dried or frozen.
- **Leeks:** Leeks are delicious when frozen or dried.

- **Peas:** Peas are best stored frozen and can keep for several months in a freezer. They can also be dried or canned.
- **Peppers:** Both sweet and hot peppers can be frozen, dried, or canned.
- **Potatoes:** Potatoes are excellent for storing and will keep for several months if stored properly. Make sure they are dry before storing them in a cool, dark area.
- **Rutabagas and Turnips:** Both rutabagas and turnips store well in a root cellar or in similar conditions.
- **Squash:** Squash is best if cured and stored in a root cellar.
- **Sun Chokes:** Sun chokes are best eaten fresh.
- **Tomatoes:** Tomatoes are great dried, canned, or frozen.

FRUIT

Berries are extremely perishable. After being picked, they will keep in your refrigerator for a week at most. Fortunately, they preserve well, and you can enjoy your strawberries, blueberries, raspberries, and blackberries year-round by freezing, making preserves, and drying them.

FREEZING BERRIES

Freezing berries is the best way to keep small fruit if diversity of use is important to you. By freezing berries whole, in slices, or as freezer jam, you can use frozen berries in most of the same ways that you use fresh berries. Here are a few different ways to freeze berries.

Tray-Freezing

The most effective and easy way to freeze whole or sliced berries is tray-freezing. Simply wash the berries in cold water, drain well, and place them in one layer on a tray or cookie sheet covered in wax or freezer paper. Once they are completely frozen, you can pack them into freezer bags. You want these bags to be packed with the same amount of looseness as the packages of frozen berries at the grocery store.

Freezing with Sugar

Frozen berries retain their texture when stored with sugar. This is also the best way to preserve berries for pies. After washing and draining your berries, coat them with sugar. Loosely pack the sweetened berries in freezer bags or other freezer-safe containers.

Freezer Jam

You can use your favorite cooked or uncooked jam recipe to make freezer jam. Simply store the jam in any freezer-safe container.

DRYING

To dry berries you will need to use a dehydrator. Drying your berries is a good idea if you have limited freezer or pantry space. Berries can be dried whole and used to cook with throughout the winter. You can also make fruit leather, which is a fun and healthy snack for kids and will last in the refrigerator for about 6 weeks.

CANNING

Canned preserves are the classic way to store berries. Canned preserves store well, are delicious, and there are many recipes that use either a single type of berry or combinations of all the berries in your harvest. If you have a pantry or root cellar, making lots of preserves is a good idea, particularly if you don't want to take up your whole freezer with berries.

No matter how you preserve your berries, there are some steps that are always used. Following is a list of tips for preserving berries.

- **Harvest:** Harvesting at the optimal time is particularly important for preserving food. It is always best to harvest berries in the morning.
- **Wash:** You should make sure berries are clean before preserving them. The best way to do this is gently, by putting berries in a bowl of cold water, allowing any dirt or particles to separate from the fruit. Either gently strain or use a slotted spoon to remove the berries from the water.
- **Quality Check:** Berries that are past their prime or slightly damaged should be separated from fresh berries in excellent condition. Use the less-than-perfect berries to make smoothies or other puréed foods. You can keep these

berries whole as long as they are cleaned, or slice them. Label the package accordingly.

Berries that are in excellent condition should be frozen whole and used in dishes where having firm berries is important, such as in pies. To keep strawberries from turning to mush, leave the hulls intact, only removing the green stem. High-quality berries should also be used when making preserves.

HERBS

Aside from their inclusion in some canning and pickling recipes, herbs are typically preserved by either drying or freezing them. Herbs that have stalks or sprigs long enough can be tied together in bunches and hung to dry. In some cases, such as preserving evergreen plants in zones where it's too harsh for them to survive outdoors in winter, the entire plant can be uprooted and hung to dry by its root stalk. Other herbs can be strung using a needle and string (smooth fishing line works well; it does not harm delicate plants). When piercing plants to string them, it's best to lead the needle through the main stalk of the plant, not the more tender leaf. This will help to keep the oils of the leaf intact, as well as prevent any dampness or pathogens from entering the leaf. The stalk is also stronger and supports the weight of the plant when it is hanging.

If you live in a humid or wet climate, you might consider using a dehydrator for tender leaves, as they can succumb to mold or dampness more easily, although not as easily as most vegetable plants because herbs lack the juices that veggies have. As a result, herbs tend to dry more successfully. After herbs are dried, gently brush or wipe off any excess dirt, and then chop and store them in an airtight container.

Most herbs are better dried than frozen, although this depends on how you plan to use them. Herbs that you plan to use for tea are almost always better dried, whereas some culinary herbs function better in their frozen form. The two most common ways to freeze herbs are by cleaning and separating the leaves and placing them in one layer on a baking sheet. Place the sheet in the freezer until the leaves are consistently frozen, then store in a freezer-safe container or bag. The second method is to wash and then cut the herbs before placing them in water in ice cube trays. Freeze the cubes and then use them by dropping them directly into cooking soups or quickly thawing before use.

APPENDIX B

METRIC/U.S. CONVERSION CHART

VOLUME CONVERSIONS

U.S. Volume Measure	Metric Equivalent
⅛ teaspoon	0.5 milliliter
¼ teaspoon	1 milliliter
½ teaspoon	2 milliliters
1 teaspoon	5 milliliters
½ tablespoon	7 milliliters
1 tablespoon (3 teaspoons)	15 milliliters
2 tablespoons (1 fluid ounce)	30 milliliters
¼ cup (4 tablespoons)	60 milliliters
⅓ cup	90 milliliters
½ cup (4 fluid ounces)	125 milliliters
⅔ cup	160 milliliters
¾ cup (6 fluid ounces)	180 milliliters
1 cup (16 tablespoons)	250 milliliters
1 pint (2 cups)	500 milliliters
1 quart (4 cups)	1 liter (about)

WEIGHT CONVERSIONS

U.S. Weight Measure	Metric Equivalent
½ ounce	15 grams
1 ounce	30 grams
2 ounces	60 grams
3 ounces	85 grams
¼ pound (4 ounces)	115 grams
½ pound (8 ounces)	225 grams
¾ pound (12 ounces)	340 grams
1 pound (16 ounces)	454 grams

OVEN TEMPERATURE CONVERSIONS

Degrees Fahrenheit	Degrees Celsius
200 degrees F	95 degrees C
250 degrees F	120 degrees C
275 degrees F	135 degrees C
300 degrees F	150 degrees C
325 degrees F	160 degrees C
350 degrees F	180 degrees C
375 degrees F	190 degrees C
400 degrees F	205 degrees C
425 degrees F	220 degrees C
450 degrees F	230 degrees C

BAKING PAN SIZES

American	Metric
8 × 1½ inch round baking pan	20 × 4 cm cake tin
9 × 1½ inch round baking pan	23 × 3.5 cm cake tin
11 × 7 × 1½ inch baking pan	28 × 18 × 4 cm baking tin
13 × 9 × 2 inch baking pan	30 × 20 × 5 cm baking tin
2 quart rectangular baking dish	30 × 20 × 3 cm baking tin
15 × 10 × 2 inch baking pan	30 × 25 × 2 cm baking tin (Swiss roll tin)
9 inch pie plate	22 × 4 or 23 × 4 cm pie plate
7 or 8 inch springform pan	18 or 20 cm springform or loose-bottom cake tin
9 × 5 × 3 inch loaf pan	23 × 13 × 7 cm or 2 lb narrow loaf or pâté tin
1½ quart casserole	1.5 liter casserole
2 quart casserole	2 liter casserole

INDEX

DISCARD